KING
Solomon

Also by Bill Crowder

Before Christmas
For This He Came
God of Surprise
Gospel on the Mountains
Let's Talk
Moving beyond Failure
My Hope Is in You
One Thing Is Necessary
Overcoming Life's Challenges
Seeing the Heart of Christ
The Spotlight of Faith
Trusting God in Hard Times
Windows on Christmas
Windows on Easter
Wisdom for Our Worries

Devotionals

A Compassionate Heart
A Present Peace

KING Solomon

Life Lessons from the Wisest Man Who Ever Lived

BILL CROWDER

Our Daily Bread
Publishing.

Interior design by Michael J. Williams

Library of Congress Cataloging-in-Publication Data

Names: Crowder, Bill, author.
Title: King Solomon : life lessons from the wisest man who ever lived / Bill Crowder.
Description: Grand Rapids, MI : Our Daily Bread Publishing, [2024] | Summary: "Learn from the person the Bible calls the wisest man who lived. In this six-chapter study by beloved author Bill Crowder, grow your Old Testament and overall biblical knowledge while also gaining valuable insights for today's decisions, relationships, and difficulties from the famous wisdom and foolishness of King Solomon. Discover how to trade pride and self-reliance for wisdom and humble dependence on God in your everyday life. "-- Provided by publisher.
Identifiers: LCCN 2023049893 | ISBN 9781640703032 (paperback) | ISBN 9781640703049 (epub)
Subjects: LCSH: Solomon, King of Israel. | Wisdom--Biblical teaching. | Bible. Kings. | BISAC: RELIGION / Christian Living / Personal Growth | RELIGION / Biblical Studies / Old Testament / Historical Books
Classification: LCC BS580.S6 C76 2024 | DDC 222/.53092--dc23/ eng/20231213
LC record available at https://lccn.loc.gov/2023049893

For Jim Moon, David Randlett, Clarence Underwood, Bob Gosselar, Gary Feenstra, Harvey Bock, and Herb Vander Lugt—men whose wisdom served as an example and a guide

CONTENTS

ACKNOWLEDGMENTS

No matter how many of these I do, two truths remain. First, writing is a solitary exercise spent in thought and in the enterprise of capturing those thoughts in print. Second, producing a book is a team effort—from the early outline and proposal approvals to the selection of a title to the editorial process to the production to the marketing. Many hands are involved, and I count myself privileged to work with the best. The team at Our Daily Bread Publishing is an outstanding bunch and have always taken my work and made it better. I am deeply thankful for all engaged in the process, but special thanks go to my editor, Joel Armstrong. Proverbs 27:17 says, "Iron sharpens iron, so one person sharpens another." This is particularly true in the relationship between writer and editor. I am thankful to have Joel helping me with my stuff but even more so to count him as a friend.

Beyond the team working to produce and market the book, all of those solitary hours of writing are made more doable by the loving encouragement of my wife, Marlene. As I type this, we are closing in on our forty-sixth wedding anniversary, and she has been the perfect partner for me in the ministry the Lord has entrusted to me. When I was a pastor, she filled the role of pastor's wife with grace and kindness, and she was and remains beloved by all who have known her. As a mom, she poured her life into our kids, and that is where the credit goes for whatever good comes out of our children—now adults with families of their own. Now, in the grandparenting stage of life, she is the apple of her grandkids' eyes. As we continue on this journey together, I am regularly astounded that the Lord would allow us to be a team and couple. I am eternally grateful.

Finally, to the only wise God, I am grateful for His many gifts. His Son, first and foremost. The Scriptures. The indwelling Spirit. The tools with which to live and engage life in a meaningful and purposeful way. Our God is truly good, and I trust He will be pleased with what is presented here.

INTRODUCTION
Studies in Contrast

*Wisdom is not a product of schooling but
of the lifelong attempt to acquire it.*

Albert Einstein

I must confess that in my growing-up years, I had a mis-shapen view of wisdom. From my young perspective, it lived in two polar opposites. As a kid I watched a lot (perhaps way too much) of The Three Stooges. Routinely Moe, the ringleader of the group, would look at Larry or Curly and sneer, "Oh, wise guy, huh?" That usually led to a smack on the head. Having two younger brothers at the time, I suspect we reenacted such a scene many, many times (with me in the role of Moe). All of this may explain why my default sense of humor is the wisecrack.

But every year at Christmas I was confronted not by wise guys but by wise men. Untold numbers of nativity scenes had the wise men, their camels, and their gifts of gold, frankincense, and myrrh. What a contrast! Men who had the wisdom and understanding to discern the Christmas star and then pursue that star in order to find Jesus. Talk about wise—but how could I do what they did?

So, as I grew older, I had this radically skewed, bipolar perspective on what it meant to be wise. Yet after coming to faith in Christ and moving into my years as a pastor, I began to observe some truly wise people and to appreciate what real wisdom looked like in the real world. As I spent time with people like Pastor Jim Moon, David Randlett, Clarence Underwood, Bob Gosselar, Gary Feenstra, Harvey Bock, and Herb Vander Lugt, I began to understand that wisdom was neither snarky (like the Stooges) nor unrepeatable (like the wise men). It was down-to-earth, practical, and productive.

As a pastor, I also learned how truly rare wisdom is in our day. As someone has said, there's nothing more uncommon than common sense. I quickly discovered how desperately I too needed the wisdom displayed by my mentors. This prompted my interest in Solomon—the wise king who became foolish. Not only in how he got wisdom but also in how he used it and ultimately how he lost it.

As we consider key moments in the life of Solomon, we will see his tremendous strengths as well as his powerful and self-destructive blind spots. Solomon's story isn't just a tale to be told. It is a cautionary tale reminding us that we too are vulnerable. We too can drift. We too can be our own worst enemies. Solomon could easily have echoed the words of the cartoon character Pogo, who famously said, "We have met the enemy and he is us."

I find this kind of study challenging, and I trust you will as well. May we together go to school on this life of profound wisdom and incredible foolishness as we consider Solomon—the wise king who became foolish. To that end, I invite you to pray with me:

Heavenly Father, how grateful we are for your wisdom, for your Spirit, and for Jesus, who became to us "wisdom from God" (1 Corinthians 1:30). Help us to live in that wisdom and protect us, we pray, from our own worst inclinations, that we might live for you. In Jesus's name we pray, amen.

1

THE RIGHT PLACE TO START

Lessons in life will be repeated until they are learned.

Frank Sonnenberg

Studying Bible characters, like any other historical figures, tells us that people are complex. They aren't one-dimensional at all but filled with paradoxes and contradictions. This is clear when we consider the characters we find in the pages of the Scriptures.

Moses was called the meekest of men (Numbers 12:3 KJV), yet he battled with massive anger issues that eventually prevented him from entering the promised land.

David was the youngest of the sons of Jesse and relegated to the care of his father's flocks, yet he stood by faith against the giant Goliath when the adult soldiers, including his older brothers, wouldn't engage the Philistine in combat. Years later, even greater contrast would be seen in David. The Scriptures describe him as a man after God's heart yet as someone capable of both adultery and murder.

Paul, a scholar of the first order and an expert in Mosaic law, seemed perfectly positioned to reach his fellow Israelites, yet he embraced the task of being the apostle to the Gentiles.

Even our Lord Himself showed profound contrast. Though He was the King of heaven, Creator of the universe, and Prince of life, as Philippians 2:5–11 explains, Jesus came as a slave and went to the cross to taste death for everyone.

This idea of contrast—even paradox—in the lives of biblical characters is also clearly displayed in Solomon. Solomon was considered the wisest man of his generation, yet his life became a vivid example of the worst kinds of foolishness.

I'm convinced that Solomon provides us with one of the great warning signs for people of our day. He reminds us how easy it is to drift. He reminds me, as hymn writer Robert Robinson put it, that I am "prone to wander, Lord, I feel it, prone to leave the God I love."

But that drifting, for Solomon, comes later. As we begin our exploration of the wise yet eventually foolish King Solomon, we find a moment of contrast at the very outset:

Now Solomon loved the LORD, walking in the statutes of his father David, except that he was sacrificing and burning incense on the high places. (1 Kings 3:3)

Notice the study in contradictions—Solomon loved the Lord, *except* . . . Here we need to remember that, unlike in our day, worship was very legislated in ancient Israel. In the West, people often change churches almost as regularly as they change outfits. In Israel, however, worship not only had defined elements; it had a defined space—the tabernacle built by Moses and the children of Israel during the early days of the exodus. Yes, 1 Kings 3:2 concedes that the people worshipped on the high places because no temple had yet been built—but they still had the tabernacle. And the high places were spaces where the pagan neighboring nations worshipped their false idols.

That tabernacle had been established as the center of Jewish life, to the extent that when the children of Israel camped in the wilderness, the tabernacle was erected first and then the tribal groups were arrayed around it in a designated order (see Numbers 2). Years later, that tabernacle was still operational into the early days of Solomon's reign. Notice 1 Chronicles 6:32:

> They were ministering in song in front of the tabernacle of the tent of meeting until Solomon's building of the house of the LORD in Jerusalem; and they served in their office according to their order.

In spite of that, Solomon, though he loved the Lord and worshipped Him, didn't worship in the prescribed place. "Solomon loved the LORD, . . . except . . ." Or, he loved the Lord, *but*. Therein is the contradiction. He loved the Lord but apparently was unwilling, uninterested, or unconcerned about how or where to express that love.

Like all of us, Solomon was a man with great strengths and dangerous weaknesses. Notice that in 1 Kings 2:46 we are told, "And the kingdom was established in the hands of Solomon." Yet his first act as king was to marry outside the nation of Israel. First Kings 3:1 begins, "Now Solomon formed a marriage alliance with Pharaoh king of Egypt, and took Pharaoh's daughter and brought her to the city of David until he had finished building his own house and the house of the LORD, and the wall around Jerusalem." This was also a direct violation of God's instructions for the Israelites, given even before they entered the promised land:

> You are to tear down their altars and smash their memorial stones, and cut down their Asherim—for you shall not worship any other god, because the LORD, whose name is Jealous, is a jealous God—otherwise you might make a covenant with the inhabitants of the land, and they would prostitute themselves with their gods and sacrifice to their gods, and someone might invite you to eat of his sacrifice, and you might take some of his daughters for your sons, and his daughters might prostitute themselves with their gods and cause your sons also to prostitute themselves with their gods. (Exodus 34:13–16)

Not only did Solomon take a foreign woman for his first wife (which, by the way, wasn't an issue about ethnicity; the law was a warning against being lured into idolatry), but he was also worshipping on the high places where the surrounding peoples had worshipped their false gods. He loved the Lord . . . but.

Even at the start, Solomon was a man of significant contradictions. And, at least in part, his weaknesses mirrored those of his father, David. So if we're to start at the beginning of Solomon's story, we must examine his backstory, and that includes part of the account of King David.

Context

Second Samuel 12 describes the birth of Solomon, the second son of David and Bathsheba, the widow of Uriah the Hittite. The previous chapter recounts David sexually taking Bathsheba while her husband—one of David's mighty men—was away at war. Which ironically was where David should've been as well.

The tale of David and Bathsheba is well-worn and well-known. In 2 Samuel 11:1 we read:

> Then it happened in the spring, at the time when kings go out to battle, that David sent Joab and his servants with him and all Israel, and they brought destruction on the sons of Ammon and besieged Rabbah. But David stayed in Jerusalem.

Why is this so important? Because the king of Israel basically had three primary roles. First, he was to administer the kingdom. Second, he was to arbitrate interpersonal disputes. Third, and of most importance for this discussion, he was to lead the armies of Israel into battle. However, when it was time to go to battle, David stayed home and sent Joab, his general, to lead the army. He was shirking his royal responsibilities.

When he observed Bathsheba and her beauty, he took her sexually. As king, he was shirking his responsibility militarily while at the same time abusing his royal authority for his personal pleasure. As king, from a human perspective, he could legally take whatever—or in this case whoever—he wanted. But what is legal is not always right, particularly in God's eyes. When Bathsheba found that she was pregnant, David eventually had her husband, Uriah, killed. When the baby died, David and Bathsheba once again got pregnant, this time with Solomon.

Upon his birth, he was named Solomon ("peace") by David, but he was also given a second name—Jedidiah ("friend of God")—by Nathan, the prophet who had confronted David's sin and cover-up of that sin.

It should be remembered that David had at least eight wives and several concubines. From these wives David had more than ten sons, all of whom could theoretically claim the throne as son of the king.

As we enter 1 Kings, David's life was waning (1:1). In an odd partnership, Bathsheba and Nathan teamed together to make certain that Solomon succeeded David on the throne (vv. 11–40)—and Solomon's rule would become Israel's golden age of peace and prosperity.

To launch such an era, where do you start? Now we turn our attention fully to Solomon.

The Prayer of Solomon (1 Kings 3:6–9)

Christopher Hitchens, a writer, social commentator, and anti-theist, said: "The man who prays is the one who thinks that god has arranged matters all wrong, but who also thinks that he can instruct god how to put them right."

Clearly that view of prayer is held by many who see no importance in it, and sadly it's sometimes the way prayer is practiced by many Christ followers. I would suggest that a much healthier and more scripturally solid view of prayer was expressed by one of America's most beloved presidents, Abraham Lincoln:

> I have been driven many times upon my knees by the overwhelming conviction that I had nowhere else to go. My own wisdom and that of all about me seemed insufficient for that day.

Where do you start? You start with prayer—and that is where Solomon started. In Gibeon (about five miles north of Jerusalem), as Solomon began his rule, God appears to the young king in a dream and offers him the opportunity to ask for whatever he wants (1 Kings 3:5). This is the first of four occasions when Yahweh speaks to Solomon (also 6:11–13; 9:1–9; 11:11–13). In response, Solomon prays:

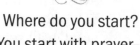

Where do you start? You start with prayer— and that is where Solomon started.

> You have shown great faithfulness to Your servant David my father, according as he walked before You in truth, righteousness, and uprightness of heart toward You; and You have reserved for him this great faithfulness, that You have given him a son to sit on his throne, as it is this day. And now, LORD my God, You have made Your servant king in place of my father David, yet I am like a little boy; I do not know how to go out or come in. And Your servant is in the midst of Your people whom You have chosen, a great people who are too many to be numbered or counted. So give Your servant an understanding heart to judge Your people, to discern between good and evil. For who is capable of judging this great people of Yours? (3:6–9)

Interestingly, in 1 Kings 2:6 and 9, David had already declared that Solomon was a wise man. Arguably, however, Solomon's greatest display of wisdom was the wisdom to pray for wisdom! That pursuit aligns with the counsel Solomon would later give to his own sons, as he wrote:

Wisdom is the principal thing;
Therefore get wisdom.
And in all your getting, get understanding.
Proverbs 4:7 NKJV

Here, given a blank check from God, Solomon asked for wisdom. What would I ask for? What would you ask for? To consider seriously the answer to that question could be self-revelatory, and not necessarily in a good way!

Notice how *The Expositor's Bible Commentary* unpacks this blank check:

> God had accepted his sacrifices and indicated his approval. The offer God made to Solomon was as much a test of character as it was a willingness to do for him whatever he wished. It served to demonstrate where Solomon's priorities lay.

In his prayer, Solomon acknowledged two important things: God's kindness to his father, David (v. 6), and Solomon's own inadequacies (v. 7). Here is wisdom. Solomon knew his weaknesses and sought God's provision to compensate for those weaknesses. He said, "I am like a little boy." Again, *The Expositor's Bible Commentary* teases out that idea for us very well:

> The term "little child," or young lad, relates both to his relative youth and to his inexperience in government. Solomon demonstrated commendable humility, and indeed the task before him was daunting. Only a fool would have entered into the kingship with a carefree and arrogant attitude. The responsibilities facing Solomon were all the greater in that Israel was God's chosen nation. Only if he were armed with wisdom

from God would he be able to govern in a manner that would lead his people in God's ways. As king and shepherd (a common designation for a king [Jer. 23; Ezek. 34]), he was responsible for their spiritual welfare as well as for their economic and political well-being.

Solomon's response to God's offer showed a deeply held sense of reliance upon God—perhaps rooted in his awareness of how God had so often provided for David. That is the heart of Solomon's starting point—praying to the God of all wisdom and asking Him for the wisdom he himself lacked for the task ahead.

What would this much-needed wisdom look like?

The Wisdom from Above (James 3:17–18)

I had just finished speaking at a Bible conference themed on Solomon and wisdom. As the attendees filtered out of the auditorium for their break, a man came to me and said, "Do you know the difference between wisdom and knowledge?" I asked him to continue and he said, "Data is knowing there is such a thing as a tomato. Knowledge is knowing that a tomato is a fruit. Wisdom is not putting a tomato in a fruit salad." We both chuckled and he exited for the break with the rest, but his layered approach to the subject was, I thought, quite helpful on a practical level. However, for our discussion of wisdom, we need something more substantial than fruit salad—and the Bible provides it.

I'm sure most who are reading this are familiar with the fruit of the Spirit in Galatians 5:22–23: "But the fruit of the Spirit is love, joy, peace, patience, kindness, goodness, faithfulness, gentleness, self-control; against such things there is no law." As such, what we're effectively being given is the evidence of a life controlled by the Spirit.

In James 3, we see a different but related kind of fruit—the evidence of a life controlled by "wisdom from above." This is what Solomon was praying for when he asked God for an "understanding heart." He wouldn't have known that this was the "fruit of wisdom," but he was praying for it nonetheless. To appreciate the kind of wisdom Solomon sought—and the kind we need as well—a glimpse into the New Testament will prove very useful. And, fittingly, it comes from arguably the most Jewish book in the New Testament—James, an epistle highly regarded for its practical wisdom.

But the wisdom from above is first pure, then peace-loving, gentle, reasonable, full of mercy and good fruits, impartial, free of hypocrisy. And the fruit of righteousness is sown in peace by those who make peace. (3:17–18)

Notice those characteristics are evidence of a life led by true wisdom—wisdom that is, in fact, from above—and we can easily imagine how each element would be useful in leading a nation. Or a family. Or living in a relationship. Or in a church. Or a workplace.

These evidences of from-above wisdom are beautifully winsome and remarkably practical. Every piece of this wisdom offers help and balm to an agitated, fractured, friction-filled situation. Think about it . . .

Pure, peace-loving, gentle, reasonable, merciful, full of good fruits, impartial, sincere.

Let's sit with this list for a moment and consider the implications of each facet of the fruit of wisdom.

Pure: James not only starts the list with "pure" but states that it is necessarily *first*. Why? The word "pure" is based on the Greek root *hagios*, which means "holy." I would suggest that wisdom is first pure because it aligns with God's holy nature and purposes, which in a sense undergird the rest. The Jamieson, Fausset, and Brown commentary explains it this way: "Literally, 'chaste,' 'sanctified': pure from all that is 'earthly, sensual (animal), devilish' (Jas 3:15). This is put, '*first of all*,' before 'peaceable' because there is an unholy peace with the world which makes no distinction between clean and unclean." The foundational element of wisdom from above is that it reflects the character and heart of the God of wisdom.

Peace-Loving: Again, this desire for peace must be measured against a desire to be in harmony with God's holiness. In *The Expositor's Bible Commentary*, George Guthrie writes, "That it is 'peace-loving' (*eirēnikos*) marks this wisdom as conducive to healthy relationships and again places it in contrast to the earthly wisdom that spawns disorder." In James 4, the writer goes on to address a conflict within the church family there—and that conflict could arguably be resolved by the institution of this aspect of wisdom.

Gentle: In Greek, *epieikes*. This can also be translated as "considerate of others." It reflects a genuine desire to show kindness to other people. This aspect of wisdom clearly stands in opposition to the worldly wisdom described in verse 16, which promotes "jealousy and selfish ambition."

Reasonable: This is the only place in the New Testament where this word is found, and it carries with it a willingness to be persuaded. It doesn't reflect a mind so open that it will accept anything and everything but one that is willing to hear the other side of an issue and weigh its merits.

Merciful: The idea of mercy is that we have compassion

for those in need—even as our God has shown mercy to us. Some say that it isn't just the feeling of concern but that mercy activates a practical response to the hurt and pain of another. As I write this, over fifty thousand people have lost their lives in a massive earthquake in Turkey and Syria, and the evidence of mercy has been the near-global response to the needs of the survivors. Among Christian responses, the ministry of Samaritan's Purse has shipped untold levels of support with staff, medical supplies, food, and more. That is mercy.

Full of Good Fruits: Why do "good fruits" appear on this list? Perhaps to line up with Jesus's words that, while we are unable to see into people's hearts, we "will know them by their fruits" (Matthew 7:20). Our lives display in actions, words, and deeds the true condition of our hearts. James, in this same chapter, already made a similar point, focusing specifically on our words: "Does a spring send out from the same opening both fresh and bitter water? Can a fig tree, my brothers and sisters, bear olives, or a vine bear figs? Nor can salt water produce fresh" (James 3:11–12). The fruit generated by our lives can either dishonor our Lord or bring Him honor (see John 15:8).

Impartial: This again reinforces an idea James has already introduced as he argued for fairness and justice (2:1–13). Being fair-minded in a world of chronic injustice is a radical idea!

Sincere: This is the term *anypokritos*, or "free of hypocrisy." To be without hypocrisy is to be genuine or authentic, another characteristic that is vital to healthy relationships.

This is the nature of a life dominated by divine wisdom, or as James put it, "wisdom from above." No wonder the person practicing such wisdom can well and truly be seen as a peacemaker, for James 3:18 summarizes these ideas, "And the fruit of righteousness is sown in peace by those who make peace." And, with that in mind, we remember the words of our Lord:

> Blessed are the peacemakers, for they will be called sons of God. (Matthew 5:9)

This is what Solomon sought—and what each of us desperately needs as we live in a broken and fractious world. In broken and fractious families. In broken and fractious churches.

Yes, in times like these we need a Savior. But in times like these we also need our Savior's powerful wisdom—and so did Solomon.

The Reply of God (1 Kings 3:10–14)

> Now it was pleasing in the sight of the Lord that Solomon had asked this thing. And God said to him, "Because you have asked this thing, and have not asked for yourself a long life, nor have asked riches for yourself, nor have you asked for the lives of your enemies, but have asked for yourself discernment to understand justice, behold, I have done according to your words. Behold, I have given you a wise and discerning heart, so that there has been no one like you before you, nor shall one like you arise after you. I have also given you what you have not asked, both riches and honor, so that there will not be any among the kings like you all your days. And if you walk in My ways, keeping My statutes and commandments, as your father David walked, then I will prolong your days."

I can't think of any more powerful words for the child of God's heart than "it was pleasing in the sight of the Lord." This powerful ideal is at the very center of what makes for a fulfilling walk of faith.

In the early pages of the Bible we are introduced to a man named Enoch—who walked with God. In the famous "hall of faith" in Hebrews 11, Enoch is described this way:

> By faith Enoch was taken up so that he would not see death; and he was not found because God took him up; for before he was taken up, he was attested to have been pleasing to God. (v. 5)

In fact, Enoch's life was so pleasing to God that he was one of only two people in the Bible (along with Elijah; see 2 Kings 2) who left this world without having to die! That is a pretty stirring endorsement for a life that pleases God.

David helps describe a God-pleasing life in his penitential psalm following his sin with Bathsheba, singing:

> For You do not delight in sacrifice, other-
> wise I would give it;
> You do not take pleasure in burnt offering.
> The sacrifices of God are a broken spirit;
> A broken and a contrite heart, God, You
> will not despise.
> Psalm 51:16–17

That is huge, given that the sacrificial system was core to Israel's practice of Judaism. Relationship with God wasn't about sacrifices—it was centered on the condition of the heart! Nowhere is this more clearly seen than in our Lord Himself, who affirmed:

And He who sent Me is with Me; He has not left Me alone, for I always do the things that are pleasing to Him. (John 8:29)

Clearly Jesus wasn't exaggerating or overstating His obedience to the Father's purposes, for God the Father declared at Jesus's baptism and again at the transfiguration:

This is My beloved Son, with whom I am well pleased. (Matthew 3:17; 17:5)

Jesus's commitment to "always do the things that are pleasing to Him" sets the bar for a meaningful and fulfilling relationship with God—and Solomon, in his first significant encounter with God, tapped into it. *The Bible Knowledge Commentary* offers helpful insight into the propriety of Solomon's pleasing request:

Solomon placed the good of God's people above his personal peace or prosperity and above any desire to become a powerful and popular king. His values were in the right place from God's perspective. Therefore God promised to give him what he requested. He would possess a wise . . . heart (v. 12) and be able to discern and render fair judgments (v. 11). Since Solomon sought what was most important God also promised to give him what was of secondary importance, riches and honor, to further enable him to govern God's people effectively. Solomon was to be the richest and most honored king of his day. If Solomon remained faithful to pursue the will of God, obeying the Law of Moses, God promised he would also live a long life.

As Solomon's life is a true study in contradictions, we know that he will eventually veer from that path. But the ending is for later. This is the beginning—and what a beginning it is! Filled with faith, hope, love, and promise, Solomon started in the right place. He began by asking for and receiving from God the wisdom he needed so very much. And, while God granted him so much more than he requested, it's Solomon's heart at the beginning of his journey as king that should captivate our attention. Our desire to please God is not to be hinged to expected outcomes but should simply be a desire to be in sync with His heart and desires.

One of my all-time favorite scenes ever filmed is in the Academy Award–winning film *Chariots of Fire*, the story of Eric Liddell, the "Flying Scotsman," and his track competitor Harold Abrahams. In the film, Liddell, who would go on to be a missionary in China, is busy preparing to run in the 1924 Paris Olympics. On a walk in the Scottish Highlands, his sister confronts him about his divided attention—wanting him to focus on preparations for missions work. Finally, Eric takes her aside and responds to her concerns, saying, "I believe that God made me for a purpose. For China. But he also made me fast. And when I run I feel his pleasure." David McCasland, who wrote a brilliant biography on Eric Liddell, maintains that scene never happened in real life—but I don't care. It speaks deeply to my heart about God and His purposes and what should be our goal. When we do, in His name, what He has made us to do, it brings pleasure to our God.

So, in our own walk with the Lord, we should also seek to please our God by aligning our prayers and desires with His good purposes. May we learn from Solomon's example and "go and do likewise" (Luke 10:37 NKJV).

The Response of Worship (1 Kings 3:15)

> Then Solomon awoke, and behold, it was a dream. And he came to Jerusalem and stood before the ark of the covenant of the Lord, and offered burnt offerings and made peace offerings, and held a feast for all his servants.

Once again, we are faced with a point of contrast. Notice that before his encounter with God, though he loved the Lord, Solomon's worship was presented wrongly on the high places. This wasn't a matter of worshipping false gods but rather was the mistake of worshipping the true God in a false way. This improper approach replicated, in a sense, the failing of Aaron and the children of Israel at the foot of Mount Sinai. When Aaron presented the people with the golden calf, he didn't say, "The God of our fathers has failed us. Here is your brand-new god!" That would've been the sin of idolatry. What he said was, "This is your god, Israel, who brought you up from the land of Egypt" (Exodus 32:4, emphasis added). This wasn't the sin of idolatry per se but rather the sin of "graven images" that Israel had been warned against in Exodus 20:4–5. Like Solomon, they were guilty of serving the true God in a wrong way.

Now, however, Solomon's first display of wisdom is seen as he leaves the high places, comes to Jerusalem, and worships in a more appropriate way—and place. Solomon goes to Jerusalem—where his father, David, had brought the ark of the covenant and where Solomon himself would soon begin construction of Israel's first temple. His request for wisdom brought an immediate impact to Solomon's thinking and practices. *The Bible Knowledge*

Commentary offers this observation on Solomon's new plan for worship:

> As is often the case, a blessing from God drew the person blessed into a closer relationship with Himself. Inspired by this revelation Solomon turned from the high place and proceeded to the divinely appointed place of worship, the tabernacle. He did not enter the most holy place; only the high priest could enter there once a year (Lev. 16). But the king stood before the ark of the Lord's covenant, outside the tabernacle facing toward the ark. Burnt offerings expressed the complete dedication of oneself to God and fellowship offerings symbolized the fellowship people can enjoy with God and with others through God's grace. Solomon's feast expressed his joy and gratitude to the members of his court.

Solomon has stepped forward—out of the shadow of his father, David, and into the confidence of God's promised wisdom for the task ahead. Without question, in spite of a couple of bumps along the way, Solomon has started in the right place—in prayer, with a sense of personal humility and dependence upon God, and in worship.

Don't Miss This!

Now, here's the amazing thing:

We can ask our God for the same thing Solomon sought.

Certainly we need wisdom as much (at least) as he did and are just as dependent upon God as he was. But there's something else. Earlier we referenced the New Testament book of James for an understanding of the character of wisdom, but in James we also find an invitation with a promise. In fact, an airtight promise with a guarantee—which is actually quite rare in the Scriptures. James 1:5 offers:

> But if any of you lacks wisdom, let him ask of God, who gives to all generously and without reproach, and it will be given to him.

In the Bible we find two kinds of promises—conditional and unconditional. In conditional promises, there is (obviously) a condition that must be fulfilled in order to receive the promise. For example, who of us doesn't want God's leading in our lives? I suspect that, at least in our best moments, we all do. So we find and quote Proverbs 3:5–6 and the wonderful promise it contains:

> Trust in the LORD with all your heart
> And do not lean on your own understanding.
> In all your ways acknowledge Him,
> And He will make your paths straight.

There it is! "He will make your paths straight." What a wonderful, blessed assurance that is. But we often overlook the three conditions that precede the promise:

> Trust the Lord with all your heart.
> Don't lean on your own understanding.
> In all your ways acknowledge Him.

Then He will make your paths straight. For the promise to be fulfilled, the conditions must be met.

Not so with the promise of Hebrews 13:5:

Make sure that your character is free from the love of money, being content with what you have; for He Himself has said, "I will never desert you, nor will I ever abandon you."

Here we find the promise of God's matchless presence in every moment of our living—no strings attached. No conditions to fulfill.

What about James's promise of wisdom? Here it is again:

But if any of you lacks wisdom, let him ask of God, who gives to all generously and without reproach, and it will be given to him. (James 1:5)

Did you hear that? God is the only wise God (Romans 16:27) and the source of all wisdom—and if we ask for wisdom, He will always give it generously. In fact, Jesus Himself came to us as "wisdom from God" (1 Corinthians 1:30). That is extraordinary!

But keep in mind that the following verse offers the condition:

But he must ask in faith without any doubting, for the one who doubts is like the surf of the sea, driven and tossed by the wind. (James 1:6)

Any of us who lacks wisdom can go to God, and He has promised to answer the prayer for wisdom if we truly trust Him to do so. This is an unbelievable gift from our God to enable us to live in this reckless, foolish, broken world.

For many years now, my favorite hymn is the hope-filled and expectant prayer "Be Thou My Vision." Among the many reasons I identify with that hymn is the second verse—a verse of reliance upon God and constant need for

His wisdom. A verse I am confident Solomon would have echoed in prayer:

> Be Thou my Wisdom, and Thou my true
>   Word;
> I ever with Thee and Thou with me, Lord;
> Thou my great Father, I Thy true son;
> Thou in me dwelling, and I with Thee one.

Questions for Personal Reflection or Group Discussion

1. Imagine for a moment that God said He would give you whatever you asked for. What would you request? Why would you ask for it?

2. Like Solomon, do you have an "except" in your walk with the Lord? "Solomon loved the Lord, . . . except . . ." If you have an except, what is it and what should you do about it?

3. What has God designed you to do? In doing that, you give Him pleasure. How is that currently taking place—or not taking place—in your relationship with God?

4. Of the characteristics of "wisdom from above" (James 3:17), which have you seen in your own life? Why can these attributes of wisdom be helpful in maintaining healthy relationships?

2

THE FIRST TEST

Any fool can know. The point is to understand.
Ernest Kinoy, "Dr. Einstein before Lunch"

I have said this before, and I usually get some odd looks when I say it: as a teacher, I really enjoyed giving tests.

Let me explain. During my senior year of Bible college, I began teaching some courses in the Bible Institute program of the school I attended. When I graduated, I joined the college faculty full-time, teaching Bible classes and some general electives like church history, homiletics (preaching), and hermeneutics (interpreting Scripture).

To be fair, when I was a student, I usually enjoyed taking tests as well, so you can see the depth of my strangeness. Tests can be tricky because people learn differently, and different kinds of tests are better for some types of students than others. Nevertheless, as a new teacher with no real experience or training in teaching (though I had already done a fair bit of preaching), I wanted to find out how I was doing in this new role. So when I gave a test as a teacher, I enjoyed it for a different reason than when I was a student—in my mind, it was a two-way transaction.

Yes, the test told me what my students had learned, but it also revealed to me what I had taught—and how effectively I'd taught it. I felt the test was as much an examination of my teaching as it was of their learning. Tests can serve a very profound purpose—they can gauge our understanding.

Context

While the "kingdom books" of the Old Testament (Samuel, Kings, and Chronicles) cover similar material and events, they do so from very different perspectives, emphasizing different things. In this sense, they are like the New Testament gospels, all of which tell the story of Jesus but from different angles for different audiences and with different emphases.

It's helpful, in light of that, to know that 1 Kings describes Solomon's life and greatness through the events he lived out, while 1 and 2 Chronicles focus on the construction of the temple. As a result, the writer of 1 Kings verifies Solomon's receipt of wisdom with the now-famous story of the two prostitutes and the baby—a story completely omitted in Chronicles.

So let's get our bearings in the story. We know that David has died and Solomon has been appointed as his successor. This is more than a mere reminder or data point. In fact, it should grab our attention. Israel's first two kings (Saul and David) had been anointed by Samuel the prophet in a display of God's acceptance of them as Israel's new human leader. Solomon, however, wasn't anointed but was more of a political appointee through the collaborative efforts of

Bathsheba (his mother) and Nathan (the prophet) lobbying David prior to his death (1 Kings 1).

Why does this matter? As we've seen, David had multiple wives (eight are named, several others are unnamed, and he had an unknown number of concubines) and through them no less than nineteen sons! If David had died without naming his heir to the throne, chaos and civil war could've erupted to devastating effect upon the nation. While there was a brief season of unrest, soon, in part because of David's endorsement, Solomon was fully recognized as the heir to the throne and the accepted king.

In a sense, the people would've felt they could trust the first two kings because their anointings had carried a divine endorsement. How could they know their God had endorsed Solomon's leadership? By witnessing a demonstration of God's provision of divine wisdom to the new king.

As such, Solomon's divinely received wisdom (for no doubt the first of many, many times) would be tested. What would that test look like? Solomon's newly acquired wisdom was immediately put to the test in the familiar story of the two prostitutes arguing over a baby. Again, this story is omitted from 2 Chronicles, where the focus is on the temple. Here, however, it may even be that the writer of 1 Kings is specifically demonstrating evidence of Solomon's wisdom early in his reign in order to contrast it to the utter lack of wisdom he would display later in life. That is, of course, the theme of our study of Solomon—the tragedy of a wise man turned foolish.

Cultural Background

When studying the Scriptures, there are layers to the context of a particular verse or story. These include the immediate verses surrounding the text itself, the larger context of the book it's in and how that book is understood, and which Testament it's in. All those things contribute to understanding context. But at times, there's also the need to sort out issues of historical and cultural context. What was happening in the world and culture of the time in which the events took place? In terms of cultural context, there are two big ideas here that set the stage for the new king's demonstration of wisdom.

The Reality of Prostitutes: Prostitution was frowned upon in ancient Israel but was widespread nonetheless. In Deuteronomy 23:18, as Moses gave the people final instructions before entering the promised land, he said, "You shall not bring the earnings of a prostitute or the money for a dog into the house of the LORD your God as payment for any vowed offering, because both of these are an abomination to the LORD your God." This was a clear statement of God's disapproval of the practice. Yet, as was true then, while prostitution is illegal in much of the Western world today, it's still practiced in a nearly ever-present way.

The Role of the King: In ancient Israel, as we have seen, the king had essentially a tripartite role. This role included leading the armies, administering the government, and adjudicating interpersonal conflicts. These roles were very different from Israel's other two official leadership positions—priests and prophets. Priests led in the worship of the nation and served as the representatives of the people before God, while the prophets represented God before the people. As a result of the king's role in serving as a kind of final court of appeals, all citizens (including prostitutes) had access to the king. This burdensome task may have been what prompted Solomon to pray for wisdom. Remember his words:

So give Your servant an understanding heart to judge Your people, to discern between good and evil. For who is capable of judging this great people of Yours? (1 Kings 3:9)

"Who is capable of judging . . . ?" The primary concern Solomon voiced in his prayer request wasn't leading the armies or administering the government per se. His main concern was judging the people, and for good reason!

Now he receives his first real test as king and judge. So, the problem is before us . . .

The Difficult Problem (1 Kings 3:16–22)

Then two women who were prostitutes came to the king and stood before him. The one woman said, "Pardon me, my lord: this woman and I live in the same house; and I gave birth to a child while she was in the house. And it happened on the third day after I gave birth, that this woman also gave birth to a child, and we were together. There was no stranger with us in the house, only the two of us in the house. Then this woman's son died in the night, because she lay on him. So she got up in the middle of the night and took my son from beside me while your servant was asleep, and she laid him at her breast, and laid her dead son at my breast. When I got up in the morning to nurse my son, behold, he was dead! But when I examined him closely in the morning, behold, he was not my son, whom I had borne!" Then the other woman said, "No! For the living one is my son, and the dead one is your son." But the first woman said, "No! For the dead one is your son, and the living one is my son." So they spoke before the king.

What a mess. It sounds like an episode of *Judge Judy* or one of those tawdry television "courtroom" programs that drag people's dirty laundry into the view of a voyeuristic public in an alleged pursuit of justice. But, as in any legal dispute, we must consider the details of the case.

- Two prostitutes share a home with each other but with no one else.
- They each give birth to a son, three days apart.
- One baby is smothered by his mom, who then swaps her dead child for the other woman's living one.
- The mom whose baby is alive (the plaintiff) brings charges before the king, which, as we've seen, was her right in their culture.
- The other woman (the defendant) denies all of the accusations leveled against her.

Those are the basic facts of the dispute. Imagine such a case being heard by the president of the United States or the prime minister of the United Kingdom. It's shocking to say the least. Now we need to take another look at this information for possible hints that reveal the size of the challenge Solomon faces here. Notice:

- There were no other witnesses (v. 18).
- There was no one else who could've switched the babies.

41

- There was no hard evidence to support either argument.
- There was, at that time, no scientific option for determining the living child's parentage (such as DNA testing).
- There was no confession from the guilty party (the defendant).

It's a classic "she said, she said" situation, leaving no basis for the rendering of judgment. Again, what a mess! How was Solomon to respond to and reconcile a disagreement that was so difficult to unravel? Richard Patterson and Hermann Austel, in *The Expositor's Bible Commentary*, explain:

> Here was a case where there were no witnesses, so it was impossible to prove by conventional means which of the litigants had a just case. Solomon displayed his extraordinary insight into human nature as well as shocking boldness of action in exposing fraud.

It was for just this type of case that Solomon had confessed to God that he was inexperienced and uninformed and needed divine wisdom to execute his tasks as king (v. 9).

Bereft of any means of discovering the truth of the situation if left to himself, Solomon would have been hopeless in trying to untie this Gordian knot of treachery and untruth. But, as we saw in chapter 1, we aren't left to ourselves. Remember what James wrote:

> But if any of you lacks wisdom, let him ask of God, who gives to all generously and without reproach, and it will be given to him. (James 1:5)

Well, Solomon had asked for wisdom from God. God has promised the provision of that wisdom. Now, in the midst of this testing situation, we—along with the nation of Israel—will discover whether or not God kept His promise.

The King's Response (1 Kings 3:23–27)

For my second pastorate, Marlene and I took the kids and moved to Southern California. While friends from West Virginia drove our things cross-country in a rental truck, we flew into Los Angeles International Airport. My secretary, Patty, picked us up there, and we dropped Marlene and the kids at the lovely rental home the church had secured for us. Patty and I then headed to the "church" so that I could get started.

On our arrival, we saw on the front door of the building a tag sealing the door and a notice from the city saying that the church building—actually a rented commercial space—was not zoned to be a church and never could be. The notice continued that unless "a representative of the organization" was in the city offices before the end of the business day, the city was shutting us down. I should've known there were challenges ahead, because when we'd left the airport earlier, the car in front of us had a bumper sticker that read, "Welcome to California. Now go home."

This was my first day on the job, so I headed to the city offices and told them I had just gotten off a plane—quite literally—and pleaded for some time to get up to speed on the situation, and that request was granted. What a first day!

As we consider the case before the new king, this is

Solomon's proverbial first day on the job, and what a situation faces him! In the midst of accusations and deceptions, it's fascinating to see how much emotion is involved and how the responses are weighted by it.

> Then the king said, "The one says, 'This is my son who is living, and your son is the dead one'; and the other says, 'No! For your son is the dead one, and my son is the living one.'" And the king said, "Get me a sword." So they brought a sword before the king. And the king said, "Cut the living child in two, and give half to the one and half to the other." But the woman whose child was the living one spoke to the king, for she was deeply stirred over her son, and she said, "Pardon me, my lord! Give her the living child, and by no means kill him!" But the other woman was saying, "He shall be neither mine nor yours; cut him!" Then the king replied, "Give the first woman the living child, and by no means kill him. She is his mother."

So, then, how do you respond to this? To set this up, we need to once more remember the heart of Solomon's petition to God in verse 9. When God promised to answer Solomon's prayer, He was specifically promising a response to the young king's request for an "understanding heart," which can be translated as "a hearing heart." What does it look like to have a hearing heart? If I'm honest, it involves a lot of stuff that I'm not very good at. I'm good with facts and information but am somewhat lacking in the emotional side of things.

A hearing heart includes sensitivity, emotional intelligence, and a high degree of insight into human nature. Much of those things comes simply by listening.

As a general rule, we learn more when we're listening than when we're talking. Surprisingly, one of the greatest guitarists of the 1960s, Jimi Hendrix, wisely said:

Knowledge speaks, but wisdom listens.

Or, as quoted at the beginning of this chapter, "Any fool can know. The point is to understand."

What a valuable insight that is! And it's clearly helpful. In facing this difficult test case, Solomon has to hear these two women, and in particular he must hear more than just their words. He must hear their hearts. And as he does, I would suggest that he is listening for

- the emotions of the two women, which help to reveal . . .
- the motives of the two women, which help to reveal . . .
- the truth of the matter.

After receiving the facts of the case with his hearing heart, the king gives his shocking judgment—kill the child! *The New Bible Commentary* points out:

The ruling is so shocking in its brutality that it sounds like the callous response of a judge wearied beyond endurance by the claims and counter-claims of the two women. Indeed, the narrative is open to that interpretation. However, the very different reactions of the women allow Solomon to decide which was the real mother of the living child. Its life is spared, and Solomon's reputation is made.

Indeed, it appears that Solomon was seeking to provoke the maternal instincts of the true mother—exposing the ultimate fact of the case. Clearly the key is the emotional responses of the two mothers, for, with the actual mother in particular, this is much more than just a test case or an intellectual exercise. As a mother, her heart is crushed with the burden of concern for her newborn son.

Where the one mother reveals her true heart by saying she would rather see the child dead than for her rival to have it, by contrast the actual mother can only think of the welfare of the child—whether he stays with her or not. James Smith observes in *The Books of History*:

> The real mother, the plaintiff as it turned out, was emotionally stirred by the decision which in effect would leave her son dead. In desperation she cried out to the king to spare the child and give it to her rival. She preferred to lose her case and see her rival rewarded than to have the child killed.

This is what Solomon's hearing heart discerned—and it makes sense. First Kings 3:26 tells us:

> The woman whose child was the living one spoke to the king, for she was deeply stirred over her son, and she said, "Pardon me, my lord! Give her the living child, and by no means kill him!"

The key phrase is "deeply stirred," which translated literally means her "bowels yearned." In the ancient Hebrew culture, the bowels (or even the womb) were considered the seat of emotions. We use similar thinking today when we say, "I just had a gut feeling." The true mother was stirred in her deepest being, displaying her actual motherhood of the disputed child. The wisdom of God gave Solomon's hearing heart insight into the radically different hearts of the two women—and a correct solution.

This was a thorny issue to be sure, but elements of the wisdom from above that we saw described in James 3 in the previous chapter rose to the surface in Solomon's verdict:

Peace-Loving: His decision brings an end to the conflict between the two women who, it seems, were friends in the past.

Reasonable: It's sensible that Solomon would seek out the heart of the true mother.

Merciful: Solomon's decision shows mercy to the actual mother by restoring her child to her.

Full of Good Fruits: Administering justice is certainly "good fruit" from a good heart—and, by means of God's imparted wisdom, Solomon does just that.

Impartial: By exposing the truth of the matter, Solomon shows he isn't siding with the woman but rather with the truth.

Sincere: A genuine, just decision is made by a wise king.

Now, with the women's hearts exposed, Thomas Constable describes the results in *The Bible Knowledge Commentary*:

Significantly the essence of wisdom is revealed in Solomon's handling of this difficult case. The king had insight into basic human nature (in this case, maternal instincts) that enabled him to understand why people behave as they do and how they will respond in various situations. The opposite of this ability is seen in simply judging people's superficial words and actions.

> Solomon had been put to the test and passed that test through the provision of God's wisdom.

Solomon had been put to the test and passed that test through the provision of God's wisdom. As a test to show his worthiness as king, this revealed to the people Solomon's fitness to lead God's people. His stressful "first day on the job" presented him with a hugely difficult test—but the divinely promised gift of wisdom was displayed, verifying that Solomon had God's endorsement for his rule.

The People's Response (1 Kings 3:28)

> When all Israel heard about the judgment which the king had handed down, they feared the king, because they saw that the wisdom of God was in him to administer justice.

> Solomon's verdict and the way it was achieved spread like wildfire, and the people held him in great awe. Here was clear evidence to an unusual degree of a God-given ability to rule with great discernment. (*The Expositor's Bible Commentary*)

Even without modern technology to pave the way, word of Solomon's verdict dashed across the country, and the people's response carried several important components.

What Was Their Response? "They feared the king." This means they looked on him with a sense of awe. They marveled at his judgment and the wisdom that was at its source.

Why Was That the Response? "Because they saw that the wisdom of God was in him to administer justice." This is the key. Solomon may not have had a prophetic anointing, but he clearly was anointed with divine wisdom. Here was a man who could be trusted to bring justice in difficult situations. Here was a man who was blessed with true "wisdom from above" (James 3:17).

Now, let's think about this story. The woman whose child was living had a profound problem and a serious need. Where could she turn? She only had one recourse—the king. And the king exercised remarkable wisdom to come to her aid and help her in her difficult situation.

Where does that leave us?

Quite simply, we also have a King. Paul wrote a profound doxology to his young son in the faith, Timothy:

Now to the King eternal, immortal, invisible, the only God, be honor and glory forever and ever. Amen. (1 Timothy 1:17)

And in Revelation 19:16, Jesus is revealed to the apostle John this way:

On His robe and on His thigh He has a name written: "King of Kings, and Lord of Lords."

Yes, we have a King—and not just *a* King but *the* King of Kings. His wisdom is not derived from another. He's the one who has become to us "wisdom from God" (1 Corinthians 1:30)! Our King can be trusted with all that we bring to Him as well. As pastor and Bible teacher Warren Wiersbe wrote:

> The fact that these two women had access to the king's throne shows how much young Solomon loved his people and wanted to serve them. How wonderful it is that every Christian has access to the throne of one who is "greater than Solomon" (Matt. 12:42), and who promises to give wisdom and to meet every need.

Let me briefly apply all this to the church situation I mentioned at the beginning of this chapter. We committed with our landlord to follow the necessary processes required by the city but were turned down on every appeal. As a church family we prayed and sought wise counsel. Finally our last resort was to appeal to the city council.

On the night of the council meeting, most of our congregation sat in the gallery of that council hall as we waited for our situation to be addressed. Through an amazing series of divine provisions, the city council not only heard our request but granted us an exemption to the codes we were deemed to be violating and provided us with a path to retrofit the building and stay open as a church. Our truly wise King answered our prayers and granted our request—even though real estate experts and professionals had told us it was an impossible situation.

As Walter Smith wrote, when we turn to God for His wisdom in our seasons of trial and heartache, we turn to the

Immortal, invisible, God only wise,
In light inaccessible, hid from our eyes,
Most blessed, most glorious, the Ancient of
    Days,
Almighty, victorious, Thy great name we
    praise.

Questions for Personal Reflection or Group Discussion

1. Whether or not you're a parent, how can you relate to the heartache of the mother of the living child? How can you relate to the desperation of the mother of the dead child?

2. Is there someone (parent, spouse, friend, mentor, pastor) you regularly turn to for advice? What makes that person trustworthy as a source of wisdom?

3. When have you felt like you were the victim of injustice? What was that like? How could a mediator with true wisdom have prevented that injustice?

4. How can our King comfort us in seasons of injustice and provide us help in those times of need?

3

THE TEMPLE IS BUILT

Wise men talk because they have something to say;
fools, because they would like to say something.

Plato

By nature, humans are builders. Put small children on the beach and they will inevitably build a sandcastle. We build houses, cities, monuments, bridges, skyscrapers, cathedrals, and more.

In the Bible, Noah built an ark, Nimrod and others built a tower to the heavens, Abraham built a nation, Moses built a tabernacle, and Jesus is building a kingdom.

We are builders.

As children, my brothers and I, along with our buddies on Walnut Street, were constantly plundering scrap lumber to build tree houses. It's a miracle any of us survived because there was no skill or strength in those structures (and I'm using that word very generously). We would, in the summer, often sleep out in the tree houses.

When I became a pastor, two of our churches engaged in major building projects in which I was heavily involved. When Marlene and I became homeowners, we completely renovated the basements of two of our houses and added an extra room in the basement of a third.

We are builders.

However, you can take every effort, every drop of sweat, every hammered nail, every second of my building efforts, and combined together they're not a drop in the ocean compared to the scope and scale of the vision of George Vanderbilt II, whose family, among other things, controlled much of the shipping and railroad traffic of their era.

In 1889, Vanderbilt began the most ambitious private home construction project in the United States. The construction project was so extensive that it required the on-site manufacturing of some 32,000 bricks a day, and the work continued until the completion of George Vanderbilt's "summer house" in 1895—six years later! The result was the Biltmore Estate in Asheville, North Carolina. To this day, it remains the largest privately owned residence in America, with 250 rooms (including 35 bedrooms and 43 bathrooms) consuming a staggering 178,926 square feet of floor space.

We are builders.

Most of us build more modestly than George Vanderbilt, but we build nevertheless. Some say they build for personal satisfaction or necessity. Others build because they want to leave behind a monument to remind the world that they were here, long after they are gone.

Solomon now enters into his own building project—yet in one sense it was less his and more the fulfillment of the desires of his father, David. It may have been an inherited dream rather than a personal one, but it would be Solomon who built the temple—and then built some more.

Context

First Kings 6 opens with a surprisingly helpful notation:

> Now it came about in the four hundred and eightieth year after the sons of Israel came out of the land of Egypt, in the fourth year of Solomon's reign over Israel, in the month of Ziv, that is, the second month, that he began to build the house of the LORD. (v. 1)

This verse may seem to contain trivial data, but it's vital because it sets the context for the entire event, and it sets that context in several ways.

The Context of Solomon's Reign

The Bible Knowledge Commentary points out,

> This verse is one of the most important in the Old Testament chronologically because it enables one to fix certain dates in Israel's history. The dates of Solomon's reign have been quite definitely established through references in ancient writings. They were 971–931 B.C. According to this verse, in the fourth year of his reign Solomon began to build the temple. That was in 966 B.C.

The Context of Israel's History

The temple's construction is also dated back to the time of the exodus, which matches the practices of ancient kings to put their major building projects in the context of some overarching national event. *The New Bible Commentary* offers this insight:

There are probably two main reasons for this. First, it invites comparison between the two events; it suggests that the building of the temple was as significant an event in Israel's history as that which saw the birth of the nation. Secondly, by placing the temple project in its historical context, it reminds us that Yahweh is a God whose purposes are worked out in history and whose plans are often long-term. The promise of a place which "the LORD your God will choose . . . to put his Name there for his dwelling" (Dt. 12:5) took many lifetimes to find its fulfilment.

Clearly there's a sense of long-awaited fulfillment here. Notice Exodus 15:17:

> You will bring them and plant them in the
>   mountain of Your inheritance,
> The place, LORD, which You have made as
>   Your dwelling,
> The sanctuary, Lord, which Your hands
>   have established.

You'll recall that Exodus 15 is Moses's song of praise and worship that celebrated God's rescue of Israel at the Red Sea. Yet woven into the lyrics of this spontaneous praise song was a prophecy of Israel's future hope and home. Moses declared that God would plant the people on the mountain of their inheritance—the place God had chosen for His dwelling and sanctuary.

With the people now fully settled in the land of promise, this prophecy must also be fulfilled with the building of a sanctuary to be Israel's place of worship and the center of their national life. It's fitting that the construction of Israel's first temple was so tightly connected to God's deliverance of them as a worshipping people.

The Work Begins (1 Kings 6:2–3)

And the house which King Solomon built for the LORD was sixty cubits in its length, and twenty cubits in its width, and its height was thirty cubits. The porch in front of the main room of the house was twenty cubits in length, corresponding to the width of the house, and its width along the front of the house was ten cubits.

If you've ever been involved in a building project, you understand the phases or stages of such a project. First, of course, is the planning stage. This is the phase where blue-sky dreaming is tempered by financial realities. Second is the materials stage—where you actually have to purchase the building supplies you will use. And once again the financial realities rear their ugly head, because it seems that most projects cost twice as much as expected. The third phase is the actual beginning of the work. There can be a bit of an excited buzz connected to this step. Finally something is being done. The fourth phase is the fatigue stage. Fatigue is almost an inevitability because not only do most building enterprises cost twice what you planned for, but they regularly take twice as long as you were hoping. Finally comes the completion stage—which includes the dreaded cleanup process. By the time you get to that point, you're so exhausted that you don't even feel like celebrating the completion of your building.

Long story short—building is a process. In fact, it's a *long* process that can induce such discouragement along the way that you feel like quitting. At that point you're almost more willing to leave the project partway done rather than spend one more dollar or one more hour on it. This is why HGTV has a program entitled *Help! I Wrecked My House*. It's about folks who throw in the towel and bring in contractor Jasmine Roth to fix the problems they've created during their home improvement efforts so that she can bring the project to completion. Where was she when I hit the discouragement phase of my last few home renovations? Yes, all of this is flowing out of years of experiences trying to improve parts of our houses—usually the basements.

As we reenter Solomon's story, the planning and materials stages are past (actually having been done by David) and the work has begun. But, much more than any simple home remodel or even the building of a new home, the construction of the temple was complex for a variety of reasons. Primarily, even the basic blueprints of the temple connected it to Israel's past—especially, again, to the exodus.

When He rescued Israel from Egypt, God led the people to Mount Sinai, where several important things took place. First, God reintroduced Himself to His chosen people. Second, the law was given to transform this people from a massively large extended family into a nation. That law primarily was given to instruct them on how to relate to their God and to one another. Third, part of the national covenant between Israel and their newly embraced God was that they would, in fact, be a worshipping people. Notice the opening portion of the Ten Commandments, given by God to Israel as they gathered at the base of Mount Sinai:

> Then God spoke all these words, saying,
> "I am the LORD your God, who brought you out of the land of Egypt, out of the house of slavery.
> "You shall have no other gods before Me.

"You shall not make for yourself an idol, or any likeness of what is in heaven above or on the earth beneath, or in the water under the earth. You shall not worship them nor serve them; for I, the LORD your God, am a jealous God, inflicting the punishment of the fathers on the children, on the third and the fourth generations of those who hate Me, but showing favor to thousands, to those who love Me and keep My commandments.

"You shall not take the name of the LORD your God in vain, for the LORD will not leave him unpunished who takes His name in vain.

"Remember the Sabbath day, to keep it holy. For six days you shall labor and do all your work, but the seventh day is a Sabbath of the LORD your God; on it you shall not do any work, you, or your son, or your daughter, your male slave or your female slave, or your cattle, or your resident who stays with you. For in six days the LORD made the heavens and the earth, the sea and everything that is in them, and He rested on the seventh day; for that reason the LORD blessed the Sabbath day and made it holy." (Exodus 20:1–11)

Not only was worship a primary focus of the Decalogue (the Ten Commandments), but that call to worship and serve the one true God also introduced a building project—the construction of the aforementioned tabernacle, a portable place of worship. This tabernacle was designed to be both literally and figuratively the center of Jewish community life. When the wandering throngs of Israelites would stop somewhere in the wilderness (as directed by the movement of the pillar of cloud by day or the pillar of fire at night), the tabernacle would be erected, and then in prescribed order the twelve tribes of Israel would establish camp around it in their designated places (Numbers 2).

Spiritually, however, the tabernacle was the centerpiece of life because it represented God's very presence in the midst of His people. In fact, when the tabernacle was first erected in Exodus 40, God established it as the place of His presence for the people:

> Then the cloud covered the tent of meeting, and the glory of the LORD filled the tabernacle. And Moses was not able to enter the tent of meeting because the cloud had settled on it, and the glory of the LORD filled the tabernacle. Throughout their journeys, whenever the cloud was taken up from over the tabernacle, the sons of Israel would set out; but if the cloud was not taken up, then they did not set out until the day when it was taken up. For throughout their journeys, the cloud of the LORD was on the tabernacle by day, and there was fire in it by night, in the sight of all the house of Israel. (vv. 34–38)

For forty years in the wilderness and then from the time of the judges to the days of Saul and finally David, the tabernacle was the designated place for this worshipping people to worship their God. Now this portable tabernacle was to be replaced by a permanent structure. And, like the tent before it, the temple would be the center of Jewish life. This is reflected in the simple fact that the dimensions for the primary building of the temple made it exactly twice the size of the earlier tabernacle. *The Expositor's Bible Commentary* explains:

> The temple (lit., "house") is here the main, central structure of the temple complex. Its dimensions were

sixty cubits long by twenty wide by thirty high. (The cubit varied somewhat but may for most general purposes be considered approximately eighteen inches in length. . . .) It was exactly twice the size of the tabernacle proper.

While we don't need to be overly concerned with the specs or the construction process of that first temple, it's vitally important that we do understand its purpose. For the people of Israel, this much larger, much more elaborate, and much more ornate temple was to once again be the center of Jewish life—because it housed the ark of the covenant, which represented God in their midst. The God who was the true and clear center of their national life would be symbolized by this temple—and, as with the tabernacle before it, they were to order their lives around the temple. As a result, three times a year the Jewish people would travel from far and wide to Jerusalem for the three main feasts (Passover and Firstfruits in spring, Tabernacles in fall; see Deuteronomy 16:16). Three times a year, life would pause for the pilgrimage to Jerusalem for these feasts, with the temple serving as the center of all the action.

This spiritual value for a physical place becomes apparent in God's second call to Solomon.

Solomon's Second Call (1 Kings 6:11–13)

Now the word of the LORD came to Solomon, saying, "As for this house which you are building, if you will walk in My statutes and execute My ordinances and keep all My commandments by walking in them, then I will fulfill My word with you which I spoke to David your father. And I will dwell among the sons of Israel, and will not abandon My people Israel."

This is the really big idea here. Even though the construction of the temple would give a center to Israel's national and spiritual life, it was always only a symbol of what mattered most. The temple could only represent the presence of God among His people—it could never truly be a substitute for it.

This is the point of God's second call to Solomon—it's a reminder of what matters most. There was value in the temple and the religious rituals carried out there, but the God who gave His people cause for worship and was a true object for their worship was always the first priority. God reminded Solomon of that here by repeating this conditional promise:

> The temple could only represent the presence of God among His people—it could never truly be a substitute for it.

- IF (the condition) you walk in My commands . . .
- THEN (the promise) I will fulfill My word to David in you . . .
- AND (the promise extended) I will dwell among the people of Israel.

Again, God's continuing presence with His people is the critical thing here. As *The Bible Knowledge Commentary* points out:

During the temple construction God reaffirmed to Solomon . . . the promise He had previously made to David. "The promise" given David to which God referred (v. 12) was that He would "establish the throne of [David's] kingdom forever" (2 Sam. 7:13). God would do this through Solomon if Solomon would obey Him (1 Kings 6:12).

Notice also the progression of the promise. Solomon, as king and David's son, has the responsibility to lead the way, but the results of the promise will affect all of Israel—not just him. *The New Bible Commentary* addresses this priority well:

> The conditional nature of God's promise to David, already made clear by David in 2:4, is now restated by God himself in words which relate it to the temple-building project. God will *live among the Israelites* if Solomon will walk in God's statutes and obey his commands. In other words, the building of a temple will not guarantee God's presence among his people; God cannot be tamed and kept in a box, however magnificent the box might be. His presence depends on obedience and specifically now on the obedience of Solomon. While these verses stop short of criticizing the building of the temple, they do put the project in perspective by stressing the larger issue of obedience.

That perspective is the key. The temple was always a representation of God's presence . . . but it needed to be seen that way and that way only. By the time we arrive in the New Testament, however, the Lord Himself had been supplanted by ritual, religious activity, and a slavish adherence to Moses's law. The trappings of religion had overtaken the presence of God Himself in the actions of the religionists.

Here, in 1 Kings 6, we find the beginning of the danger,

for with physical representations of the invisible God comes the danger of even the temple itself becoming an idol.

The Work Is Finished (1 Kings 6:14, 37–38)

So Solomon built the house and finished it. . . .

In the fourth year the foundation of the house of the LORD was laid, in the month of Ziv. In the eleventh year, in the month of Bul, that is, the eighth month, the house was finished in all its parts and in accordance with all its plans. So he was seven years in building it.

The Expositor's Bible Commentary frames the completion this way:

Seven years were required to complete the temple. An enormous amount of labor and a lavish expenditure of funds were involved. All the plans and specifications of David were carried out. It must have been a moment of great satisfaction to Solomon to see the fulfillment of his father's dream; and when God acknowledged the temple by filling it with his glory, Solomon's joy knew no bounds.

The result? Not fatigue or relief, as I described in my own modest building endeavors, but worship was Solomon's response to completing the house of God in Jerusalem.

The Worship of God (1 Kings 8:54–61)

When Solomon had finished praying this entire prayer and plea to the LORD, he stood up from the altar of the LORD, from kneeling on his knees with his hands spread toward heaven. And he stood and blessed all the assembly of Israel with a loud voice, saying:

"Blessed be the LORD, who has given rest to His people Israel in accordance with everything that He promised; not one word has failed of all His good promise, which He promised through Moses His servant. May the LORD our God be with us, as He was with our fathers; may He not leave us nor forsake us, so that He may guide our hearts toward Himself, to walk in all His ways and to keep His commandments, His statutes, and His ordinances, which He commanded our fathers. And may these words of mine, with which I have implored the favor of the LORD, be near to the LORD our God day and night, so that He will maintain the cause of His servant and the cause of His people Israel, as each day requires, so that all the peoples of the earth may know that the LORD is God; there is no one else. Your hearts therefore shall be wholly devoted to the LORD our God, to walk in His statutes and to keep His commandments, as at this day."

As Solomon and the people of Israel celebrated the completion of the temple, there are some important ideas that rise to the surface here.

- **The Posture of Worship**. "Kneeling on his knees with his hands spread toward heaven . . . he stood" (vv. 54–55). From kneeling in prayer to standing in worship, Solomon inclined both body and heart to God.
- **The Praise of Worship**. "Blessed be the LORD, who has given rest to His people" (v. 56). The key here is "rest." In Deuteronomy 12:9–10, rest was described as

Israel's living in security in the land of promise. In the following verses, Israel was told to bring her sacrifices to the place where God would cause His name to dwell (meaning the future temple). Then the people would rejoice before the Lord (v. 12). There can be no doubt that Solomon saw the temple as the completion of the picture of rest portrayed in Deuteronomy 12.

- **The Prayer of Worship.** "May the LORD our God be with us" (v. 57).
- **The Purpose of Worship.** ". . . so that all the peoples of the earth may know that the LORD is God" (v. 60).

Even in the Old Testament, part of the reason for worship was to demonstrate to the watching world the matchless character of our God! And how did God respond? With His presence! His presence consecrated that place as it had done with the tabernacle in Exodus 40.

Now when Solomon had finished praying, fire came down from heaven and consumed the burnt offering and the sacrifices, and the glory of the LORD filled the house. (2 Chronicles 7:1)

Worship has ever and always been about celebrating the person and presence of God . . . and the same is true for us, for as our Immanuel, Jesus came to be "God with us" (Matthew 1:23)! Notice that in the beginning, the first man and woman enjoyed the unfettered presence of God in the garden (Genesis 2)—but that was disrupted by sin. Then, as Warren Wiersbe put it:

God originally dwelt in the tabernacle (Ex. 40:34), then in Solomon's temple. The glory of God then came to earth in the Person of Christ (John 1:12–14). Today, every true Christian is the temple of God (1 Cor. 6:19–20), as is the church collectively (Eph. 2:21) and locally (1 Cor. 3:16).

And, in the eternal state, it gets even better! Revelation 21:22 (NIV) tells us:

I did not see a temple in the city, because the Lord God Almighty and the Lamb are its temple.

No temple made with human hands can substitute for the uncreated Creator, who is the maker of all things!

————————

One of the realities of sports is that teams or franchises have peaks of greatness and valleys of indifference (at best) or misery (at worst). The 1980s were the glory years of the Boston Celtics, who are now, after years of struggle, once again relevant. The 1980s were also the best years for the San Francisco 49ers, who have never since reached the same level of greatness. In baseball, the Big Red Machine (the Cincinnati Reds) of the 1970s is a fading memory, while the pennants the Pittsburgh Pirates won in the "We Are Family" era seem a long, long time ago.

Peaks and valleys. We know that all of us experience peaks and valleys in our lives, not least of all in our walk with God. Hymn writer William Orcutt Cushing wrote of the valleys:

> Down in the valley with my Savior I would
> go,
> Where the storms are sweeping and the
> dark waters flow;

With His hand to lead me I will never,
    never fear,
Dangers cannot fright me if my Lord is
    near.

Follow! Follow! I would follow Jesus!
Anywhere, everywhere, I would follow on!
Follow! Follow! I would follow Jesus!
Everywhere He leads me I would follow
    on!

Peaks and valleys. Ups and downs. Highs and lows. This is the stuff of which life is made and part of what makes life so challenging.

Why does this matter?

In this chapter, we've seen what is essentially the peak of Solomon's walk with God. He will still have moments, but after the building and consecration of the temple in Jerusalem, it is pretty much downhill. This is Solomon at his best, as his commitment to honor his God by finishing the task entrusted to him by his father, David, sees the temple fully realized.

This is Solomon at the mountain peak. He has performed this dramatic spiritual task of temple building, he has heard again from God, and he has reaffirmed his commitment to his God. But sadly, as we saw at the beginning of this book, that mountain peak will be followed by a serious set of valleys that will impact not only Solomon but the nation as well.

Later Solomon's disobedience resulted in God's removing part of the nation from the control of his son Rehoboam. God also promised that if Solomon obeyed the Lord his nation would enjoy God's fellowship and protection. Israel experienced this only partially because of Solomon's later apostasy. (*The Expositor's Bible Commentary*)

Is there a message in here for us as followers of Christ? I think there's both a message and a warning. The message is that, like everything else in the Old Testament, this points to Jesus. The tabernacle—that rough tent in which God's presence dwelt among His people—pointed forward to the earthly, physical body in which Jesus came to be among His people. In his great theological prologue to his gospel, the apostle John wrote:

And the Word became flesh, and dwelt among us; and we saw His glory, glory as of the only Son from the Father, full of grace and truth. (1:14)

The key here is that the word "dwelt" is the Greek term *eskenosen*, which translates "tabernacled." As the tent of meeting was a temporary dwelling place for God, so Jesus came and tabernacled in human flesh for a brief period of time.

Now the warning. Like Solomon, it's easy for the rituals and buildings and tasks of the life of faith to crowd out the presence of God from our lives. As for Solomon, heavy activity in good work can become a substitute for the God who alone should be the object of our passion and desire. The things we do can become gods that distract our hearts from the true and living God. In fact, rather than being consumed with the physical trappings of church and ministry, Paul pushes us to an even higher reality:

Or do you not know that your body is a temple of the Holy Spirit within you, whom you have from God, and that you are not your own? For you have been bought for a price: therefore glorify God in your body. (1 Corinthians 6:19–20)

The third person of the Trinity lives within us! We are His temple, and as such, our walk with God, communion with God, and desire to live out His words must ever and always be the priority of our living, as Warren Wiersbe rightly cautioned:

How tragic that the Jews trusted the presence of their temple instead of the promises of the Lord; for in less than 500 years, this temple was destroyed as the Jews went into captivity for their sins. In 6:11–13, God reminded Solomon that the important thing was obeying His Word, not building a great temple.

Solomon's temple was a majestic building, but it was ultimately only a building that would be ransacked and destroyed. We must lift our eyes higher, beyond temples and tasks, buildings and building. We must look to the God whose presence gives meaning to all that is done in His name. As Elisha Hoffman penned:

> What have I to dread, what have I to fear,
> Leaning on the everlasting arms?
> I have blessed peace with my Lord so near,
> Leaning on the everlasting arms.
>
> Leaning, leaning,
> Safe and secure from all alarms;
> Leaning, leaning,
> Leaning on the everlasting arms.

Questions for Personal Reflection or Group Discussion

1. Have you ever been involved in a construction or home improvement project? Was it rewarding or frustrating? Why?

2. Why was the temple so central to Israel's worship and national identity? How did the building of the temple show Solomon at his best?

3. Whereas the temple symbolized God's presence among His people, Jesus came in a physical body to literally be Immanuel—"God with us." How does that promise and reality offer you comfort in hard times?

4. How have you seen God's help carry you through some of the valleys of life? How might that encourage you to trust Him in future trials?

4

THE FAME SPREADS

Who is like the wise?
Who knows the explanation of things?
A person's wisdom brightens their face
and changes its hard appearance.

Solomon (Ecclesiastes 8:1 NIV)

Modern-day Yemen is the second-largest nation on the Arabian Peninsula, covering an area of about 214,000 square miles and boasting a population of almost thirty-five million. Found on the southern edge of the Arabian Peninsula, Yemen, known in Roman times as Felix Arabia (meaning "Happy Arabia"), is a challenging place to live. Yemen is well described on one United Nations web page this way: "Since 2011, Yemen has been in a state of political crisis starting with street protests against poverty, unemployment, corruption, and president Saleh's plan to amend Yemen's constitution and eliminate the presidential term limit." Due to this extreme poverty and unrest, Yemen isn't necessarily a hugely attractive tourist destination—but what tourism does take place is often directly attached to archaeological and historical studies.

Why?

Because, for some three thousand years, Yemen was at the crossroads of various civilizations—bringing it a large measure of prosperity. Also in ancient times, Yemen was the home of the Sabean Kingdom—which some say came into existence as early as 12000 BC. As the base of the Sabean Empire, ancient Yemen was the home of the queen of Sheba (not Ethiopia or Egypt as is often presented in film). As such, she traveled some twelve hundred miles from ancient Yemen to Jerusalem to make a rather dramatic appearance in the Scriptures in her now-famous visit to King Solomon.

So, humanly speaking, why would the narrator include this account as part of the larger Solomon story? Remember that, as we saw earlier, the writers of Chronicles presented Solomon's greatness through the construction of the majestic temple in Jerusalem. The author of Kings, however, used historical events—like the conflict between the two prostitutes—to display the wisdom and influence of Israel's great king.

To that end, recording the events of the visit of foreign royalty to test Solomon's wisdom and see his grandeur fits perfectly into that approach. While flattering, this becomes a kind of beginning of the end as the king's heart starts the slow process of turning away from God. As *The Bible Knowledge Commentary* tells us:

> This incident seems to have been included here to support the statements made previously that Solomon's reign was so glorious that rulers from all over the world came to see his kingdom and observe his wisdom (4:34). Its function is similar to the story of the two prostitutes (3:16–28) which also illustrated Solomon's wisdom. Interestingly both stories pertain to women, though of different social strata.

So, let's explore together this historic visit and see its impact on both Solomon and the queen of Sheba.

The Visit Begins (1 Kings 10:1–2)

Now when the queen of Sheba heard about the fame of Solomon in relation to the name of the LORD, she came to test him with riddles. So she came to Jerusalem with a very large entourage, with camels carrying balsam oil and a very large quantity of gold and precious stones.

Who was she? The Scriptures don't give us her name, but history tells us, rather ambiguously, that she was one of several queens in southern Arabia. When you remember that the Sabean Empire was over a thousand miles from Israel, two things are remarkable. First, it's remarkable in the technology-less ancient world that the rumors of Solomon's greatness and wisdom had traveled so far. Second, it's fascinating that she was so impressed by the rumors she'd heard that she packed up what must've been an enormous entourage to make the long, difficult, and time-consuming journey to Jerusalem just to see if the rumors were true. *The New Bible Commentary* explains it this way:

A more straightforward translation would be that she had heard of "the fame of Solomon concerning the name of the LORD." While this might refer to the temple, it more probably sums up everything which Solomon had achieved, for he had achieved it as the ruler appointed and empowered by Yahweh.

That's impressive.

What is most impressive about her visit may be this fact

that her primary area of concern had to do with Solomon's relationship with his God. Notice verse 1, which says that she wanted to explore "the fame of Solomon in relation to the name of the LORD." Yes, as verse 2 continues, she was planning to test Solomon's wisdom, but the rumor that appears to have captured her imagination wasn't simply the greatness of Solomon. As *The Expositor's Bible Commentary* puts it:

> What is noteworthy is that his fame was associated with his relationship to the name of the Lord. His fame was a testimony to the greatness of God. . . . The Hebrew construction "makes God the focus for both Solomon's wisdom and his reputation."

God was the focus of Solomon's reputation, and that reputation—rooted in his relationship with the God of Abraham, Isaac, and Jacob—had reached to the far corner of southern Arabia in such compelling fashion that the queen of Sheba had to see it for herself.

> God was the focus of Solomon's reputation, and that reputation . . . had reached to the far corner of southern Arabia in such compelling fashion that the queen of Sheba had to see it for herself.

For Jerusalem, it must've felt like they were being invaded! In verse 2 we're told that she came "with a very large entourage." What would that have entailed? Well, the text tells us this retinue included "camels carrying balsam oil and a very large quantity of gold and precious stones." I would suggest that the key phrase is "a very large quantity." Not only would it have taken numerous camels to carry that much weight, but there would've undoubtedly been some troop of soldiers to protect the caravan. Remember, in the ancient world, travel was not only arduous and challenging; it was also dangerous. An unguarded caravan would've been an attractive target for bandits or highwaymen. Additionally, it's unlikely this queen would've traveled without a staff of attendants and, particularly, her personal bodyguard team. The text doesn't tell us how large the "very large" retinue was, but it's not exaggerating to say it could've numbered in the hundreds of people, with many, many animals!

This was no small enterprise. So then, what drove the queen of Sheba to go to such an extent to visit a fellow sovereign—in fact, one she had never met?

The Visit's Purpose (1 Kings 10:1–3)

> She came to test him with riddles. . . . When she came to Solomon, she spoke to him about everything that was in her heart. (vv. 1–2)

Some commentators say this trip was probably a trade mission in which the queen of Sheba sought to negotiate with Solomon, because Israel controlled the north-south trade routes. While that may have been part of it, the narrator tells us her motivation, for she came to test Solomon with "riddles." *The Expositor's Bible Commentary* offers helpful background on these riddles:

> [These] were enigmatic sayings or questions that cloaked a deeper philosophical, practical, or theological truth. Arabic literature abounds in riddles and proverbs. They were a favorite sport and a way to test one's mettle. It would appear from the following

verses that the "riddles" or "hard questions" posed by the queen were not merely frivolous tests of mental quickness but a genuine seeking for truths hidden in some of the enigmatic sayings known to her.

One commentary states that this sort of testing was a kind of sport among ancient Near Eastern monarchs. Clearly she was testing Solomon to prove the legitimacy of his now-famous wisdom. But, as I stated earlier, this seems to be more than simply sport. Notice that verse 2 also tells us she "spoke to him about everything that was in her heart." She wasn't just testing him with random riddles or obtuse questions but was pursuing higher truth—perhaps seeking some spiritual bearings by which to direct her own life and rule.

In the winter of 2023, a spiritual revival broke out at Asbury University—a private Wesleyan-based Christian college in Wilmore, Kentucky. The resulting revival went on for several weeks, and fed by reports circulating on social media, people traveled from all over America to witness for themselves what they had heard about in rumor.

I would suggest that this is both highly unusual and not all that unusual at the same time. While it seems unusual for people to take the time and go to the expense to explore a rumor, what isn't unusual is that something seen from a distance could awaken a sense of spiritual hunger in people. At its essence, that was why people traveled to Asbury, and I'm convinced this was at the core of the queen's trip to Jerusalem. Like the wise men who would follow the star in pursuit of Israel's newborn king, she followed the beacon of Solomon's reputation, and it led her to Jerusalem, where she could find answers to her questions.

This is also the kind of spiritual hunger that was part of

my own motivation to attend a newly established Christian college in 1973. Out of a desire to seem cooler, I told friends and family I was going to the school to play football and find a wife, but there was also a spiritual hunger that had been awakened in my heart when my dad and I visited the campus months earlier. During that visit, we talked to staff and students and attended a church service that was unlike anything I had ever been part of—despite having grown up going to church. This was different and I was captivated by it. And two months after I started classes at the college, I came to know Christ as my Savior—the ultimate satisfaction to my spiritual quest.

In this respect, I appreciate and identify with the queen of Sheba. Her journey was neither easy nor without cost. Neither was mine, though the cost was expressed in very different ways. Nevertheless, it was a journey well worth taking—and I'm certain the queen of Sheba felt the same way. Notice verse 3:

> Solomon answered all her questions; nothing was concealed from the king which he did not explain to her.

We aren't told what her religious leanings were before coming to Jerusalem, but it's clear she was open to spiritual wisdom and insight. We're also not told what her specific questions were, but whatever they were, they were all answered to her satisfaction. At the very least, she was on the same path Solomon longed for his own sons to take when he wrote:

> To know wisdom and instruction,
> To discern the sayings of understanding . . .
> Proverbs 1:2

A Powerful Impression (1 Kings 10:4–7)

It's been said that the root of all disappointment is unmet expectations. We all know how that feels, right? We spend months planning a party or wedding or project or vacation, and in the end we're too often frustrated that it wasn't all that we had hoped it would be.

By the same token, when something exceeds our expectations, it can take our breath away. I remember, as a diehard supporter of Liverpool Football Club, the first time I was able to attend a match at Anfield Stadium—Liverpool's home ground. It was amazing. The energy in the stands as the fans roared their heroes on was unlike anything I'd ever experienced in American sports. The most special moment, however, had little to do with football (or what Americans call soccer). In England particularly, most teams have a song or anthem that the fans sing to the players before the start of the match, and Liverpool's anthem is poignant—"You'll Never Walk Alone." It's a message from the supporters to the team and coaches that we're all in this together. Win or lose. As forty-five thousand Liverpool supporters rose to sing at the top of their voices, the hair on the back of my neck stood up. It was a rare moment of spectacle that I'll never forget. And it thoroughly exceeded my admittedly high expectations.

The queen of Sheba traveled over a thousand miles to see if Solomon and his wisdom could live up to the expectation his reputation had set for her. Was she disappointed in what she encountered in Jerusalem? The narrator answers that question unequivocally:

When the queen of Sheba saw all the wisdom of Solomon, and the house that he had built, and the food of his table, the seating of his servants, the service of his waiters and their attire, his cupbearers, and his burnt offerings which he offered at the house of the Lord, she was breathless. Then she said to the king, "It was a true story that I heard in my own land about your words and your wisdom. But I did not believe the stories until I came and my own eyes saw it all. And behold, the half of it was not reported to me. You have exceeded in wisdom and prosperity the report which I heard."

Not only was she not disappointed—her doubts and skepticism were blown apart! She arrived at Jerusalem as a self-confessed skeptic and left convinced of the greatness of Solomon's God-given wisdom. That wasn't all of it, however. Notice the extent of what impressed her so:

Solomon's wisdom

The house he built (speaking here of his home, not the temple)

The food he ate (obviously food fit for a king)

The seating of his servants

The service of his waiters

The attire of his waiters

His cupbearers

The burnt offerings he offered at the temple (not to mention the grandeur of the temple itself!)

Talk about drinking from a fire hydrant! Everywhere the queen of Sheba looked, she saw something that took her breath away (v. 5). I can't begin to imagine the degree to which she must've felt overwhelmed. Richard Patterson and Hermann Austel, in *The Expositor's Bible Commentary*, describe the scene this way:

> This last idea is rendered literally "there was no more spirit left in her," indicating extremely strong emotion. This expression is used in Joshua 2:11 and 5:1 of the dismay and consternation experienced by the Canaanites at the coming of Israel, not because of the strength of Israel's army but because of the evident miraculous working of God in their behalf. "Dismay" would not be correct here, but she was totally undone (NIV, "overwhelmed") with amazement.

As Alfred Edersheim wrote in *Bible History: Old Testament*,

> It was this scene of wealth and magnificence, unexampled even in the East, as well as the undisputed political influence and supremacy of the king, combined with the highest intellectual activity and civilization in the country, which so much astounded the Queen of Sheba on her visit to Solomon's dominions.

In ancient times, when a degree of splendor wasn't unusual in palaces and throne rooms, the scene in Solomon's kingdom was beyond imagination. In verse 7 we are given the queen's final assessment of what she experienced. To paraphrase her words, she saw Solomon, his wisdom, and his splendor as far surpassing all the extravagant rumors she had heard. She wouldn't have believed it, but having seen it with her own eyes, she can't deny Solomon's greatness.

Parting Words and Gifts (1 Kings 10:8–10)

"Blessed are your men, and blessed are these servants of yours who stand before you continually and hear your wisdom! Blessed be the LORD your God who delighted in you to put you on the throne of Israel; because the LORD loves Israel forever, He made you king, to do justice and righteousness." Then she gave the king 120 talents of gold, and a very large amount of balsam oil and precious stones. Never again did such a large quantity of balsam oil come in as that which the queen of Sheba gave King Solomon.

It's not unusual when world leaders congregate or meet on a personal visit that they share gifts with one another. The website for the John F. Kennedy Presidential Library describes the gifts given to President and Mrs. Kennedy on display in the White House Corridor exhibit of the library:

Gift-giving between foreign leaders is an important part of international relations. President and First Lady Mrs. Kennedy received gifts from 106 different heads of state from all over the world. On display are a selection of these ceremonial gifts that were presented to the Kennedy White House as symbols of diplomacy in an exhibit that recreates the White House corridor.

The exchange of gifts among heads of state is a centuries-old tradition, and remains a part of the culture of modern-day international relations. President and First Lady Jacqueline Kennedy delighted in the gifts presented to them by representatives of countries around the globe, particularly items which showcased the fine work of a foreign country's craftsmen. In both the Oval Office and the rooms of the White House, the president and first lady would display such gifts for visitors to enjoy.

When you consider that Kennedy was only president for three years, it's amazing to think that 106 world leaders bestowed gifts upon them during that brief time. This centuries-old tradition of gift-giving even went back to ancient times and the queen of Sheba's visit to Solomon. Her gifts consisted of both words and wealth.

Her Words

Her first words were a statement of recognition that Solomon's people were blessed to be in his presence and have constant access to the king's wisdom. She said, "Blessed are your men, and blessed are these servants of yours who stand before you continually and hear your wisdom!" There may even be a hint of jealousy on her part—she had only the opportunity for this brief visit, but they were in Solomon's presence all the time!

Her words, however, also hint at the spiritual pursuit we suggested earlier. She said, "Blessed be the LORD your God who delighted in you to put you on the throne of Israel; because the LORD loves Israel forever, He made you king, to do justice and righteousness."

In both statements, she uses the word "blessed," but in Hebrew they are two different words. When she speaks of Solomon's men, she uses the word *asre*, which means "happy." However, when she speaks of God, she uses the word *baruk*, which means "to praise." In essence, she is blessing (praising) God for blessing Israel with a king like Solomon. So profound is the gift of such a king that she declares it to be evidence of the Lord's love for Israel forever

(v. 9). She also reminds Solomon of the sacred trust he has been given to "do justice and righteousness" among the people God loves so deeply.

These are not mere words of praise or empty flattery. They're the overflow of an overwhelmed heart—a heart that has had its expectations exceeded beyond imagination.

Her Wealth

In verse 10, the queen of Sheba gives Solomon 120 talents of gold and more balsam oil and gemstones than the nation of Israel had ever received before. What an extravagant gift!

It's helpful to remember that in Old Testament times, wealth wasn't measured in coin or currency but rather by weight. Think of the term *pound*, used for British currency. It's also a measurement of weight, and the word itself actually means "weight." So, if wealth was measured by weight, how much was a talent?

The Bible Knowledge Commentary says that 120 talents of gold was approximately four and a half tons! As I write this, the value of gold per pound is $22,372. This means that the queen of Sheba's gift to Solomon was in excess of $200 million in today's money ($201,348,000)—not counting the precious jewels and balsam oil. Talk about a parting gift.

It's important to note that Solomon reciprocated as well. The narrator explains this in verse 13:

> King Solomon granted the queen of Sheba everything she desired, whatever she requested, besides what he gave her in proportion to his royal bounty. Then she departed and went to her own land together with her servants.

No doubt her camels were just as heavy-laden on the return journey as they had been on arrival in Jerusalem. If the author's purpose in including this story was, in fact, to display Solomon's greatness, then this is clearly mission accomplished. Not only did the people of Israel bear witness to his greatness, but foreign dignitaries did as well.

One additional thing to consider: There have been suggestions over the years of a sexual tryst between Solomon and the queen of Sheba, particularly in film and television. Such a suggestion may be logical based on Solomon's expansive relationships with women. In fact, there have been eleven different films about the queen of Sheba and Solomon and five television productions. Most present a romantic connection between the two. This, however, is nothing but speculation. The entire story of their encounter is before us in 1 Kings 10, and there isn't the faintest hint of an affair between the two sovereigns.

I find this compelling because the Scriptures aren't shy about telling us of Solomon's sexual proclivities (as we'll see later). If such a relationship existed between Solomon and the queen of Sheba, it's hard to imagine that piece of the tale being left out. While some rabbis speculated of such an affair and Islamic tradition proposes that the two married, the biblical account is silent on all such issues.

So then, where does this leave us? Perhaps once again with the reminder that we have an even greater King than Solomon. In Luke 11:31, Jesus said to the listening crowd:

> The Queen of the South will rise up with the men of this generation at the judgment and condemn them, because she came from the ends of the earth to listen

to the wisdom of Solomon; and behold, something greater than Solomon is here.

In his *The Bible Exposition Commentary*, Warren Wiersbe, one of my favorite Bible teachers, shed valuable light on Jesus's words:

> The emphasis here is on the wisdom of a king, not the works of a prophet. The Queen of Sheba traveled many miles to hear the wisdom of Solomon (1 Kings 10), but here was the very Son of God *in their midst*, and the Jews would not believe His words! Even if Jesus had performed a sign, it would not have changed their hearts. They needed the living wisdom of God, but they were content with their stale religious tradition.

The queen of Sheba blessed the God of Israel for giving Israel a wise king. How much more should we bless our God for giving us the wisest of all kings—Jesus Himself! Who could ask for more? With a life of dependence on Him and His wise guidance, we can echo the words of beloved hymn writer Fanny Crosby:

> All the way my Savior leads me;
> What have I to ask beside?
> Can I doubt His tender mercy,
> Who through life has been my Guide?
> Heav'nly peace, divinest comfort,
> Here by faith in Him to dwell!
> For I know, whate'er befall me,
> Jesus doeth all things well;
> For I know, whate'er befall me,
> Jesus doeth all things well.

Questions for Personal Reflection or Group Discussion

1. Have you ever visited a place of royal splendor? If so, what was that like? What grabbed your attention? If not, what comes to mind when you think of displays of royal wealth?

2. When you hear rumors of greatness in some realm of life (sports, music, teaching, etc.), do you tend to be skeptical or accepting of those rumors? When has your skepticism been challenged by the facts that proved the rumors true?

3. Think of a time when you received a spectacular gift. How did that make you feel about the giver of that gift?

4. Do you have a spiritual hunger that could lead you to pursue a spiritual movement? Why or why not?

5

THE DANGER GROWS

*The saddest aspect of life right now is that science
gathers knowledge faster than society gathers wisdom.*

Isaac Asimov

We live in the age of consumerism, where marketing and advertising drive us to want what we
don't need and to buy what we can't afford. But
in this time of abundance and plenty, can you have too
much of a good thing? Opinions vary:

Too much of a good thing is just about right. (Jerry
Garcia, The Grateful Dead)

Too much of a good thing can be wonderful. (Mae
West, actress)

Can one desire too much of a good thing? (William
Shakespeare, "As You Like It")

If one is good, ten are better. (Anonymous)

However, Aesop, of fables fame, said rather bluntly, "It
is possible to have too much of a good thing." Why would

that be? Several possible reasons occur to me on this difficult subject.

A life of excess can create resentment, jealousy, and friction in relationships with those whose lives are less fortunate, as well as a feeling of entitlement that we really should be able to have whatever we want whenever we want it.

There is wisdom in the biblical call to moderation, where life is lived in balance rather than in excess (see Philippians 4:5 KJV). The common sense of seeing the danger even of too much good food fits here, and too much bad food creates a very different set of problems—as evidenced in the provocative film from several years ago *Super Size Me*.

Too much of a good thing can impact our values, both spiritually and materially. As the old B. J. Thomas song challenged us, we are to use things and love people—not the other way around.

In his book *The Call*, which is my all-time favorite book outside the Bible itself, Os Guinness tells the story of John D. Rockefeller Sr., who, when asked how much money it takes to make a man happy, gave the immortal reply, "Just a little bit more." Too much of a good thing? In Rockefeller's case, it was more like never enough.

Also in *The Call*, Guinness tells the story of the artist Eugène Delacroix, who once asked James de Rothschild, of the powerful banking family, to pose for a painting of a beggar since he had "exactly the right hungry expression." Rothschild, who was a friend of the artist, agreed and appeared the next day, suitably garbed in a disreputable costume. The masquerade was so convincing that a passerby on the street even stopped and gave the banker some money.

Out-of-balance excess can create a kind of insatiability that becomes the driving force of a life in pursuit of "more, more; faster, faster." Now, don't misunderstand me: this isn't a call to asceticism, nor is it a condemnation of things. It's simply a reminder that as followers of Christ, we aren't called to consumptive consumerism, but rather we are called to contentment—and too much of a good thing can quickly become the enemy of contentment. As 1 Timothy 6:6 (NKJV) reminds us:

Now godliness with contentment is great gain.

This brings us back to King Solomon. Blessed by God with great wisdom, Solomon also enjoyed extraordinary wealth and possessions—and, like the wisdom he received, these came from God's hand. Remember from chapter 1 that when God offered Solomon a proverbial blank check, Solomon asked for wisdom. Now remember too God's response:

I will do what you have asked. I will give you a wise and discerning heart, so that there will never have been anyone like you, nor will there ever be. Moreover, I will give you what you have not asked for—both wealth and honor—so that in your lifetime you will have no equal among kings. (1 Kings 3:12–13 NIV)

Solomon was blessed by God with matchless wisdom but also with enormous wealth—and that formed the seed of the problem, for as someone wisely said, "It takes a steady hand to hold a full cup." Possessing can be one of life's greatest tests of character. With his cup full to overflowing, Solomon's hands will begin to lose their steadiness, and it will happen because arguably he has too much of too many good things.

The Extravagance of Wealth (1 Kings 4:22–25)

When I was in Bible college, one of the subjects that occasionally came up in casual conversation was the "desert island" problem, as in, "If you were trapped on a desert island in the middle of the ocean, what would you want with you?" That may seem like a silly question, especially so many years before the Tom Hanks movie *Cast Away*, but if for a moment you take it seriously, it may help you to sort out where your values are.

So how would you answer the question? You probably wouldn't place a priority on your phone, your TV streaming subscriptions, or your golf clubs. More likely you would focus on fresh water, needed medications, and sustainable food. Perhaps in a whimsical moment you might even pick a few good books to sustain you mentally for the duration of your time there.

The question is interesting because it forces us to distinguish between wants and needs, and once again that brings us back to Solomon. While most of us have fairly modest day-to-day needs, Solomon's daily provision was nothing short of incredible, as the narrator of 1 Kings tells us:

Now Solomon was ruling over all the kingdoms from the Euphrates River to the land of the Philistines and to the border of Egypt; they brought tribute and served Solomon all the days of his life.

Solomon's provision for one day was thirty kors of fine flour and sixty kors of meal, ten fat oxen, twenty pasture-fed oxen, and a hundred sheep, besides deer, gazelles, roebucks, and fattened geese. For he was ruling over everything west of the Euphrates River, from Tiphsah even to Gaza, over all the kings west of the

River; and he had peace on all sides surrounding him. So Judah and Israel lived securely, everyone under his vine and his fig tree, from Dan even to Beersheba, all the days of Solomon. (4:21–25)

I think that, clearly, the key phrase here is in verse 22, "Solomon's provision for one day." For *one day*. ONE day. In order for us to appreciate the magnitude of what this means, we need some help understanding the terminology of the ancient world. To that end, Thomas Constable explains these measurements well in *The Bible Knowledge Commentary*:

The ability of the nation to provide Solomon's daily provisions (cf. v. 7) testifies to its prosperity (vv. 22–23). Those provisions included 30 cors (30 donkeyloads or 185 bushels) of fine flour . . . 60 cors (60 donkeyloads or 375 bushels) of meal, 30 head of cattle . . . 100 sheep and goats, and wild meat (deer, gazelles, roebucks) and fowl.

Remember, that's for *one* day. To that analysis *The Expositor's Bible Commentary* adds:

[This] suggests that the number of people who could be fed by this amount of food would amount to anywhere between 14,000 and 32,000 persons. . . . The amounts are "entirely believable, and . . . there is no reason to doubt that its details are factual." It may well be that the food supported those stationed in the various garrisons as well as those connected with the palace itself.

Obviously this speaks to the overall prosperity of the nation that it could support the kind of indulgence Solomon clearly enjoyed. Perhaps this is a good time to once again ask the question, Can you have too much of a good thing? Or maybe a more provocative question, How much do you really need? This level of extravagance can be both a blessing and a curse—God blessed Solomon in extraordinary ways, but those blessings, like all blessings, were to be stewarded, not just consumed.

> God blessed Solomon in extraordinary ways, but those blessings, like all blessings, were to be stewarded, not just consumed.

I have had the privilege of knowing a few people who, as followers of Christ, were remarkably blessed financially. In my observation of an admittedly small sample size, there seemed to be very little middle ground. Either their wealth ruined them and pulled them further away from the Lord, or they were able to see their wealth as a tool to serve the Lord by serving others. Contentment produced generosity, and a lack of contentment produced an unquenchable desire for more.

To some this may seem like an unnecessarily negative approach to this aspect of Solomon's life. But I urge you to remember that while the Scriptures here are neutral about Solomon's extravagance, it isn't difficult to see that this isn't a stopping place—it's a step on a journey. And because we know where this journey will end up, we can look back and see the warning signs along the way. Consumptive materialism is one of those warning signs. Another is . . .

The Quest for Security (1 Kings 4:26–28)

"Working without a net" is a phrase that gets the attention of any circus goer who watches the trapeze artists. I remember attending the circus in Moscow some thirty years ago, and the athleticism and grace of those performers was breathtaking. What was most breathtaking, however, was the fact that they worked without a net.

Without a net speaks of the inherent danger of flying from trapeze to trapeze with no protection in the event of losing one's grip on a fellow trapeze artist or the trapeze itself.

Without a net means that with one false move the trapeze artist would come crashing to the ground below—and possibly suffer a painful death.

Without the protection and security provided by the net, disaster awaits.

Security is not a small thing. Where do we look for security? What becomes our net? In our generation, we certainly have loads of options in all arenas, personally, locally, and globally.

Personally: IRAs, 401(k)s, stock portfolios, rising salaries, retirement planning, wealth management, insurance policies, real estate

Locally: fire and police departments, hospitals and medical services, paramedic squads, neighborhood watch groups, home security systems

Globally: military might, economic dominance, significant global influence

It's important to recognize that, again, none of these things are bad or sinful or inappropriate. And, in and of themselves, none of them represent a lack of trust or confidence in God. But looking to them as our source of true security will always fall short of what our hearts really crave. We see this in a very subtle way as 1 Kings 4 continues:

Solomon had forty thousand stalls of horses for his chariots, and twelve thousand horsemen. And those deputies provided food for King Solomon and all who came to King Solomon's table, each in his month; they allowed nothing to be lacking. They also brought barley and straw for the war horses and baggage horses to the place where it was required, each deputy according to his duty. (vv. 26–28)

By any definition, this is a lot of horses and chariots! In fact, *The Bible Knowledge Commentary* reminds us that "Solomon's numerous horses (12,000; cf. 2 Chron. 1:14) and many chariots (1,400 according to 2 Chron. 1:14) were kept in several locations (called 'chariot cities' in 2 Chron. 9:25; cf. 1 Kings 9:19)."

While some debate the size of those numbers (in part because of 2 Chronicles 9:25), entire cities had to be built just to house Solomon's horses! These cities included Hazor, Gezer, and, most famously, Megiddo.

Why so many chariot cities? Because chariot cities were the hallmark of military readiness.

Why did chariots matter? Because chariots were the bleeding edge of military technology in the ancient world. Chariots were the ultimate safety net, providing national security for Israel from any and all enemies.

Admittedly, this doesn't seem like a problem. In fact, it seems to be the very essence of prudence and wise planning. But that's what we see when we look through human eyes alone. Warren Wiersbe wrote insightfully of this situation:

Solomon's kingdom was the largest in Israel's history (v. 21, and see Gen. 15:18). Those were days of peace and prosperity (v. 25). However, the seeds of sin and apostasy were being sown. Solomon brought horses from Egypt (10:26–29) in direct disobedience to the Law (Deut. 17:16). He also multiplied wives (11:1 with Deut. 17:17). These sins eventually brought ruin to the kingdom.

This is the problem. Once again, we need to travel back in Israel's history to the exodus. After forty years of wandering in the wilderness, a new generation was coming up—a different generation than the one that had received and agreed to the law of Moses at Mount Sinai. So, it made sense that before they entered the promised land, the law needed to be repeated and reinforced. Listen to what Moses told Israel as they stood on the threshold of the promised land:

> When you enter the land which the LORD your God is giving you, and you take possession of it and live in it, and you say, "I will appoint a king over me like all the nations who are around me," you shall in fact appoint a king over you whom the LORD your God chooses. One from among your countrymen you shall appoint as king over yourselves; you may not put a foreigner over yourselves, anyone who is not your countryman. In any case, *he is not to acquire many horses for himself*, nor shall he make the people return to Egypt in order to acquire many horses, since the LORD has said to you, "You shall never again return that way." And he shall not acquire many wives for himself, so that his heart does not turn away; nor shall he greatly increase silver and gold for himself. (Deuteronomy 17:14–17, emphasis added)

We may find this passage odd, yet the point was a simple one—Israel was the people of God, and He was to be seen as the source and substance of their security. For the king to begin stockpiling military hardware was in direct defiance to God's instructions and a denial of God's capabilities for protecting them. And it can't be missed that right after this warning about seeking security through military might, Israel was warned about their king accumulating multiple wives, and we know—and will clearly see—how that part of Solomon's story ends.

We live in a different time and have a different national purview than Israel did, but as individuals who, as followers of Christ, are God's people today, we should be reminded that we too must never forget the source of our real security. And it isn't financial planning or stock portfolios, good and wise though they may be. As Psalm 121:3 says, "He will not allow your foot to slip; He who watches over you will not slumber."

Our God is our security. And that reality is reinforced in the New Testament as well. Jesus said:

My sheep listen to My voice, and I know them, and they follow Me; and I give them eternal life, and they will never perish; and no one will snatch them out of My hand. My Father, who has given them to Me, is greater than all; and no one is able to snatch them out of the Father's hand. (John 10:27–29)

As the sheep of our Good Shepherd, we are doubly safe—in Jesus's hands and in the Father's hand as well. This sentiment is echoed in Martin Luther's famous and beloved hymn "A Mighty Fortress Is Our God." Based on Psalm 46, it affirms:

And though this world, with devils filled,
Should threaten to undo us,

We will not fear, for God has willed
His truth to triumph through us.
The prince of darkness grim,
We tremble not for him;
His rage we can endure,
For lo! his doom is sure;
One little Word shall fell him.

The Pursuit of Knowledge (1 Kings 4:29–33)

Extravagance of wealth. Expansion of military might. Now one more piece of the puzzle of Solomon's fame—and the growing danger it represents—is seen in his relentless pursuit of knowledge. Let me remind you of the quote that opened this chapter:

> The saddest aspect of life right now is that science gathers knowledge faster than society gathers wisdom. (Isaac Asimov)

Again, we can't stress strongly enough that knowledge, in itself, isn't evil or dishonoring to God. In fact, it can be greatly honoring to God if measured with the wisdom that Asimov saw lacking. But it's possible to be ruined by education and the pursuit of knowledge. Solomon himself would come to recognize this concern, as he expressed in Ecclesiastes 1:18:

> In much wisdom there is much grief; and increasing knowledge results in increasing pain.

So, even in the accumulation of good things—like knowledge—there can be substantial danger, as we see in Solomon's story:

Now God gave Solomon wisdom and very great discernment and breadth of mind, like the sand that is
on the seashore. Solomon's wisdom surpassed the
wisdom of all the people of the east and all the wisdom of Egypt. For he was wiser than all other people,
more than Ethan the Ezrahite, Heman, Calcol, and
Darda, the sons of Mahol; and his fame was known
in all the surrounding nations. He also spoke three
thousand proverbs, and his songs numbered 1,005.
He told of trees, from the cedar that is in Lebanon
even to the hyssop that grows on the wall; he told also
of animals, birds, crawling things, and fish. (1 Kings
4:29–33)

Again, this is God's provision, answer to prayer, and supply for Solomon. It resulted in him becoming a polymath—
a kind of "pre-Renaissance man"—because of the breadth
of his study and learning.

And, again, this doesn't have to be a bad thing. But, if
misappropriated, any blessing can become problematic, as
The Bible Knowledge Commentary explains:

This additional information about Solomon's wisdom
demonstrates God's faithfulness in blessing the king as
He had promised (cf. 3:12; 5:12). Wisdom is the ability to live life successfully. While Solomon possessed
this ability he did not always apply it to his own life.
Thus the wisest man who ever lived (i.e., with the
greatest wisdom) did not live as wisely as many others
who preceded and followed him. Having insight into
life does not guarantee that one will choose to do what
is right. Solomon's great insight was his ability to see
the core of issues (e.g., 3:16–27). His understanding

was vast; today he would be described as a man of encyclopedic knowledge.

While accumulation of knowledge can create its own problems, *The Bible Knowledge Commentary* continues its report on Solomon's knowledge by showing how it was also used well:

> Several hundred of Solomon's 3,000 proverbs have been preserved in the Book of Proverbs as well as a few in Ecclesiastes. One of his 1,005 songs is the Song of Songs. Solomon's literary output was extremely prolific. He became an authority in botany and zoology too. The statement in verse 34 is a hyperbole (an overstatement to make a point); obviously not every nation on earth sent a representative to visit Solomon. The point is that many important visitors from faraway places visited Solomon who received them openly at his court. He was recognized as the wisest man of his day.

This is an amazing testimony to the faithfulness of God. Yes, Solomon had and did all these things . . . but out of the supply that God had given.

But again, too much of a good thing can be a troubling thing. Hear Solomon's own words as he reflected on his learning and knowledge in the book of Ecclesiastes:

> I communed with my heart, saying, "Look, I have attained greatness, and have gained more wisdom than all who were before me in Jerusalem. My heart has understood great wisdom and knowledge." And I set my heart to know wisdom and to know madness and folly. I perceived that this also is grasping for the wind. (1:16–17 NKJV)

Knowledge in itself can be either a good thing or a bad thing—depending on what we do with it and what it does to us.

Does our knowledge point us to the all-knowing God?

Does our wisdom find anchor in the all-wise God?

Does our learning position us to learn of Him?

Solomon himself recounted the danger of his excessive consumption in Ecclesiastes 2, where he described his many pursuits:

Pleasure: "I said to myself, 'Come now, I will test you with pleasure. So enjoy yourself.' And behold, it too was futility. I said of laughter, 'It is senseless,' and of pleasure, 'What does this accomplish?' I explored with my mind how to refresh my body with wine while my mind was guiding me wisely; and how to seize foolishness, until I could see what good there is for the sons of mankind to do under heaven for the few years of their lives. . . . I provided for myself male and female singers, and the pleasures of the sons of mankind: many concubines." (vv. 1–3, 8)

Possessions: "I enlarged my works: I built houses for myself, I planted vineyards for myself; I made gardens and parks for myself, and I planted in them all kinds of fruit trees; I made ponds of water for myself from which to irrigate a forest of growing trees. I bought male and female slaves, and I had slaves born at home. I also possessed flocks and herds larger than all who preceded me in Jerusalem" (vv. 4–7).

Wealth: "I also amassed for myself silver and gold, and the treasure of kings and provinces" (v. 8).

Knowledge and Wisdom: "So I turned to consider wisdom, insanity, and foolishness; for what will the man do who will come after the king, except what has already been done? Then I saw that wisdom surpasses foolishness as light surpasses darkness. The wise person's eyes are in his head, but the fool walks in darkness. And yet I know that one and the same fate happens to both of them. Then I said to myself, 'As is the fate of the fool, it will also happen to me. Why then have I been extremely wise?' So I said to myself, 'This too is futility.' For there is no lasting remembrance of the wise, along with the fool, since in the coming days everything will soon be forgotten. And how the wise and the fool alike die!" (vv. 12–16).

You can hear the skepticism and dissatisfaction dripping from every verse. Solomon had more than a heart could desire—but did all that possessing and achieving bring him joy? Fulfillment? Peace? Far from it. In the end, the king offered this chilling assessment of his many humanly successful pursuits:

So I hated life, for the work which had been done under the sun was unhappy to me; because everything is futility and striving after wind. (v. 17)

The Dark Side of Prosperity

Someone might say, "Why so negative? Why take such a dark view of such wonderful gifts and blessings?" That is a point well-taken. Good food, preparations for the future, the pursuit of knowledge . . . as I've repeatedly affirmed, none of these things are evil. None of these things are essentially wrong. James 1:17 says:

> Every good thing given and every perfect gift is from above, coming down from the Father of lights, with whom there is no variation or shifting shadow.

Every good and perfect gift comes to us from our heavenly Father—and He gives us those good gifts for our benefit. But we also make choices of what we do with those provisions, and we can abuse those good gifts. We aren't that different from

> Jacob, who abused the gift of his father's trust;
>
> Samson, who abused the gift of his strength; and
>
> David, who abused the gift of his office.

Nor was Solomon. God gifted him with more than a heart could desire, but too much of a good thing can be ultimately harmful both to us and to others unless it's stewarded under God's wisdom.

Remember, we know the end of Solomon's story, and as with so many of the characters we encounter in Scripture, his is a cautionary tale. Yes, there is much good here, but as *The New Bible Commentary* observes:

> And yet there is a tension in this chapter. For when we read it in the light of later events it is hard to avoid the conclusion that the extravagance of Solomon's court, and the burden which it placed on the northern tribes,

were the seeds of that discontent which eventually split the kingdom.

Yes, seeds of discontent sown among the nation eventually resulted in a divided kingdom. When Solomon's son Rehoboam succeeded his father on the throne of Israel, the young new king foolishly accepted unwise counsel that ignited a rebellion among the people. Having served as laborers for Solomon's expansive building projects, the people rebelled against Rehoboam's threat to make their lives even harder (1 Kings 12:16) and followed Jeroboam in separating the northern tribes and forming the kingdom of Israel—leaving Rehoboam with Judah and Benjamin (v. 21).

Not only did Solomon's actions lead to resentment among the people, but they began to germinate the early seeds of spiritual failure for Solomon himself. The result of success and prosperity without proper self-awareness can be self-destruction. And the pursuit of excess in seemingly good things can bleed into other areas of life where excess is most certainly out of line. As we'll explore in our final chapter, Solomon needlessly traveled that path of excess in the area of his marriage relationships.

For all Solomon's prosperity, wisdom, and acclaim, his success lacked the governance of the heart of God—and that is a governance we should desperately pursue. May our hearts reflect the contentment of H. G. Spafford's classic hymn, which, written following the tragic deaths of his four daughters, asserts:

> When peace like a river attendeth my way,
> When sorrows like sea billows roll;

Whatever my lot, Thou hast taught me to
    say,
"It is well, it is well with my soul."

It is well (it is well) with my soul (with my
    soul);
It is well, it is well with my soul.

Whatever my lot . . . it is well. That, friends, is a heart of
contentment at arguably the worst moment of Spafford's life.

Questions for Personal Reflection or Group Discussion

1. Consider the quotes at the outset of this chapter. Do
   you think there can be too much of a good thing?
   Why or why not?
2. Why do you think humans feel so compelled to
   create their own imagined security rather than
   trusting in God for that safety?
3. If you were stranded on a desert island, what would
   you feel like you needed? Why would that be so
   necessary?
4. Spafford's hymn at the close of the chapter speaks of
   a deep spiritual contentment at a time of significant
   personal loss. Is contentment a struggle for you?
   Why or why not?

6

THE WRONG PLACE TO END

Let your fountain be blessed,
And rejoice in the wife of your youth.

Solomon (Proverbs 5:18)

One of the most profound statements I have ever encountered came from the Danish philosopher and theologian Søren Kierkegaard, who wisely said:

Life can only be understood backwards, but it must be lived forwards.

How many of us have reached a crisis moment in our lives, only to ask ourselves, "How did I ever get here?" Years ago, I was working with the Singapore office of Our Daily Bread Ministries on some publishing projects, and I developed a close relationship with the graphics director, Alex. In fact, many times when I would travel to Singapore, I stayed in Alex's home with him and his family. One day, as we were driving to the office, Alex became unusually quiet. I finally asked what he had on his mind, and he responded, "I have a question, but I don't want to offend you."

How's that for a kickoff!

I responded that we were friends and he didn't need to worry about offending me, so he presented this question: "Why are old pastors so bitter?"

I paused for a second in a rare moment of self-restraint and then said, "First of all, *as* an old pastor and on behalf of old pastors everywhere, can we start by agreeing that not all old pastors are bitter?"

We laughed together and then agreed, "But far too many are."

As I considered his question, I finally said, "I don't know why so many old pastors seem to be bitter, but I know this: none of them set out to become bitter old pastors. They went into ministry to serve God and serve people, but they nevertheless ended in a place they never intended to be."

"How did we get here?" can be a valuable and insightful question to wrestle with.

We began in the preceding chapter to consider some things that may have started or contributed to the spiritual erosion of King Solomon's heart. Now, as we conclude our brief look into the life of Israel's wisest king, we see that erosion come to its final point of deterioration. But, as Kierkegaard said, life must be understood looking backward. Remember where we started? Let's look backward and see:

Now Solomon loved the LORD, walking in the statutes of his father David. (1 Kings 3:3)

What a change has taken place! The king who loved the Lord and longed to build Him a temple eventually became a warning sign to future generations, prompting Nehemiah to say:

Did Solomon the king of Israel not sin regarding these things? Yet among the many nations there was no king like him, and he was loved by his God, and God made him king over all Israel; yet the foreign women caused even him to sin. Has it not then been reported about you that you have committed all this great evil by acting unfaithfully against our God, by marrying foreign women? (Nehemiah 13:26–27)

As *The Expositor's Bible Commentary* observes of the tragic end of Solomon's story in 1 Kings:

This section stands in stark contrast to the statement of 3:3 that Solomon loved the Lord and walked in the ways of his father, David. That fervent love for God is now diluted and even replaced by his love for his pagan wives.

What do we do with that?

Context

In an earlier chapter we discussed at length the difference between the conditional promises and unconditional promises found in the Scriptures. We now lean into that distinction and see what happened when Solomon no longer fulfilled the conditions attached to the promises he had received from God. See again God's promises to Solomon:

Now it was pleasing in the sight of the Lord that Solomon had asked this thing. And God said to him, "Because you have asked this thing, and have not asked for yourself a long life, nor have asked riches for yourself, nor have you asked for the life of your enemies, but have asked for yourself discernment to understand justice, behold, I have done according to your words. Behold, I have given you a wise and discerning heart, so that there has been no one like you before you, nor shall one like you arise after you. I have also given you what you have not asked, both riches and honor, so that there will not be any among the kings like you all your days. And if you walk in My ways, keeping My statutes and commandments, as your father David walked, then I will prolong your days." (1 Kings 3:10–14)

Clearly, the promises were attached to the condition of verse 14 that Solomon "walk in [God's] ways, keeping [His] statutes and commandments." When Solomon departed from following God, God's favor left him—and tragedy was the result. *The Expositor's Bible Commentary* explains:

God's former approval is now replaced by his disapproval. The former promise to shower Solomon with blessings as long as he remained faithful is now replaced by the announcement of judgment to come. It comes as a shock to the reader to see this giant of a king, with all his God-given abilities, now falling prey to the blandishments of idolatry.

Solomon had been given so much yet ultimately turned away from the God who'd shown so much kindness to him.

So then, how did Solomon fall so far from the position of privilege and blessing he had received from his God? Solomon had been given so much yet ultimately turned away from the God who'd shown so much kindness to him. I would suggest that, as we saw in the previous chapter, Solomon's fall wasn't like going over a cliff. It was a slow erosion over time that started with too much of a good thing and eventually found him with simply too much of everything—both good and bad.

The Slow Drift (1 Kings 11:1–8)

If you've ever played golf, you know how small the margins are between success and failure. And the higher up you go in levels of competition, the more that differential matters. When I was younger, I hit the ball pretty far—and if I mis-hit even by only a couple of degrees, that put me deeper and deeper into trouble. The farther the ball traveled, the more off target it became. When PGA Tour players mis-hit by a couple of degrees, they can miss their target by forty or fifty yards! The farther it goes, the worse it gets.

In a sense, Solomon does the same thing. He goes further and further down the wrong path—and the further he goes, the worse it gets.

> Now King Solomon loved many foreign women along with the daughter of Pharaoh: Moabite, Ammonite, Edomite, Sidonian, and Hittite women, from the nations of which the LORD had said to the sons of Israel, "You shall not associate with them, nor shall they associate with you, they will certainly turn your heart away to follow their gods." Solomon clung to these in love. He had seven hundred wives, who were princesses, and three hundred concubines; and his wives turned his heart away. For when Solomon was old, his wives turned his heart away to follow other gods; and his heart was not wholly devoted to

the LORD his God, as the heart of his father David had been. For Solomon became a follower of Ashtoreth the goddess of the Sidonians, and of Milcom the abhorrent idol of the Ammonites. So Solomon did what was evil in the sight of the LORD, and did not follow the LORD fully, as his father David had done. Then Solomon built a high place for Chemosh, the abhorrent idol of Moab, on the mountain that is east of Jerusalem, and for Molech, the abhorrent idol of the sons of Ammon. He also did the same for all his foreign wives, who burned incense and sacrificed to their gods. (1 Kings 11:1–8)

This is almost unbelievable, yet it's the true reality of Solomon's shameful fall. That fall began by ignoring the warning signs that God had established—not only for Israel's king but for Israel itself!

Warning to Israel: "You shall not worship any other god, because the LORD, whose name is Jealous, is a jealous God—otherwise you might make a covenant with the inhabitants of the land, and they would prostitute themselves with their gods and sacrifice to their gods, and someone might invite you to eat of his sacrifice, and you might take some of his daughters for your sons, and his daughters might prostitute themselves with their gods and cause your sons also to prostitute themselves with their gods." (Exodus 34:14–16)

Warning to the King: "He shall not acquire wives for himself, so that his heart does not turn away; nor shall he greatly increase silver and gold for himself" (Deuteronomy 17:17).

Now, what must be repeated here is that this issue of foreign wives isn't a matter of ethnicity—it's a call to spiritual purity for both the people and the king. Warren Wiersbe explains this clear warning:

> These warnings were at the heart of the Mosaic law's concern about intermarrying between Israel and those cultures. This was not an issue of ethnicity (all of these groups were Semitic ethnically), nor was it just prohibition for the sake of prohibition. It was totally about spiritual purity. Foreign wives brought their idols with them, and the spiritual danger that created was the heart of the command.

Nevertheless, Solomon started by making a marriage alliance with the daughter of Egypt's pharaoh (1 Kings 3:1). That, however, was only the beginning. The longer it went on, the worse it got, until Solomon ended up with

> seven hundred wives (princesses given to Solomon in political marriages to secure treaties); and
>
> three hundred concubines (a harem of women for his personal pleasure, or at least to add to his grandeur).

If that shocks you . . . it's supposed to. The reader is supposed to be stunned by the extreme degree of Solomon's disobedience. Warren Wiersbe wrote:

> It is unbelievable that the man who wrote Prov. 5:20–23 and 6:20–24 would multiply wives and concubines from heathen nations. Polygamy itself was bad enough (it had caused his father David no end of trouble), but to take wives from heathen lands was deliberate

apostasy. See Deut. 7:1–14. What was the cause of this repeated sin? Solomon's heart was not right with God (11:4). God wanted "integrity of heart" (9:4), which means a united heart single to the glory of God. But Solomon had a divided heart—he loved the world as he tried to serve God. What a tragedy that the man who built the temple to the one true God should begin to worship at heathen altars.

I remember, years ago, an interview with a movie star of great fame. The interviewer asked, "What does it feel like to know that almost any woman in the world would sleep with you? That you could have almost any woman? How does it feel to be a real man?" The actor responded, "That's not a real man. Any dog can do that. A real man is someone who can keep one woman happy for her whole life. That is a real man." Unfortunately, Solomon didn't understand that, instead accumulating wives by the hundreds.

As Moses had warned, these marriages brought spiritual entanglements, and the man who started out with a deep love for the Lord (1 Kings 3:3) became an idolater under the influence of his foreign wives. The two most grievous examples of that idolatry are listed—and, again, it's intended to shock us, as seen in the explanations provided by Thomas Constable in *The Bible Knowledge Commentary*:

Ashtoreth (11:5): "Ashtoreth was a goddess of sex and fertility whose worship involved licentious rites and worship of the stars. She was a vile goddess (cf. 2 Kings 23:13)."

Molech (v. 7): "Molech worship involved human sacrifices, especially children, which was strictly prohibited by the Law (Lev. 18:21; 20:1–5)."

Remember that one of the keys we discussed in the previous chapter was the human tendency to struggle with contentment. Having amassed unbelievable wealth, possessions, security, and luxury, Solomon clearly wasn't content with one wife (and she a foreign wife with foreign gods). Therefore, he began stockpiling wives as well. Insatiability is like drinking salt water. Not only does it not quench your thirst—it makes you thirstier!

The accumulation of a thousand wives pushed Solomon further and further from the God who had blessed him, and now he—while not totally casting God aside—added the gods of the nations to his religious retinue. *The New Bible Commentary* observes:

> This is the ultimate irony: the king who built the temple, thus making the high places obsolete, went on to build high places himself—and for the worship of other gods! Twice in these verses we are told that in behaving this way Solomon failed to live up to the wholehearted commitment shown by David (4, 6)—a requirement clearly stated in 9:4. The stage seems set for immediate disaster.

To make it all worse, this is the man who wrote to his son about the dangers of sexual entrapment and where it can lead:

> For why should you, my son, be exhila-
> rated with an adulteress,
> And embrace the breasts of a foreigner?
> For the ways of everyone are before the
> eyes of the LORD,
> And He observes all his paths.
> His own wrongdoings will trap the wicked,

And he will be held by the ropes of his sin.
He will die for lack of instruction,
And in the greatness of his foolishness he
    will go astray.

Proverbs 5:20–23

We aren't told when Solomon recorded those wise words, so it makes me wonder:

Did he write them when he was younger and living in tune with the Lord's purposes and committed to purity?

Did he write them when he was older and reflecting on his spiritual failures?

Either way, Solomon, with a life of blessing and provision from the Lord he loved, turned his back on that God—and brought disaster on himself and the nation. Simply put, he turned away from the Lord (1 Kings 11:4).

Having built a temple in Jerusalem for the worship of the one living God, Solomon now built worship sites for the false gods his wives imported into the nation—effectively legitimizing those gods as an alternative to the true God! And this didn't only impact Solomon badly:

Ignoring this injunction would not only be harmful to the person engaged in such a marriage, but it would also necessarily affect the children. In Solomon's case, his successor, Rehoboam, was the son of an Ammonite woman (14:31). If Solomon was adversely affected by his foreign wives, much more would Rehoboam be influenced by a pagan mother. (*The Expositor's Bible Commentary*)

It's important here to make an observation about what is called "generational sin." We saw in chapter 1 that Solomon's father, David, had at least eight wives and an unspecified number of concubines. Solomon's compounding of his father's sin is, I think, a clear example of God's warning to Israel through Moses in Exodus 34:6–7:

> Then the LORD passed by in front of him and proclaimed, "The LORD, the LORD God, compassionate and merciful, slow to anger, and abounding in faithfulness and truth; who keeps faithfulness for thousands, who forgives wrongdoing, violation of His Law, and sin; yet He will by no means leave the guilty unpunished, inflicting the punishment of fathers on the children and on the grandchildren to the third and fourth generations."

After describing Himself as a God of both endless love and mercy as well as a God who judges sin, the Lord makes a statement about "visiting the punishment of fathers on the children and on the grandchildren to the third and fourth generations." It's a statement that has troubled many. Why should the great-great-grandchildren suffer because of the great-great-grandparent's sin? The simple answer is that they shouldn't—which the Lord makes clear in Deuteronomy 24:16:

> Fathers shall not be put to death for their sons, nor shall sons be put to death for their fathers; everyone shall be put to death for his own sin alone.

What then is the reality of generational sin that Exodus 34:7 is talking about? I think there are two ways that the parent's sin can be visited on the following generations.

First, there can be consequences of sin that stretch

forward for many years to come, and the ensuing generations may bear the brunt of that. Imagine for a moment that Adolf Hitler and Eva Braun had married sooner and had children. Can you imagine how difficult it would be to live life as Hitler's granddaughter or grandson in a post–World War II, post-Holocaust world? Sin can be forgiven but consequences remain. In Solomon's case, some of those generational consequences arrived when his son Rehoboam took over the kingdom.

Second, there can be harmful consequences of the example that has been set. As the saying goes, history doesn't repeat itself, but it rhymes. In this case, Solomon's life rhymes with David's because he followed his father's bad example of polygamy—even aggravating that failing by multiplying foreign wives whose gods, as God had warned, drew Solomon's heart away from the God who had so wonderfully blessed him.

So, where would Solomon go from here? Into the loving discipline of the God he abandoned.

The Loving Discipline (1 Kings 11:9–13)

I remember many times when, as a child, I misbehaved and was disciplined by my parents. Back in those olden times, spanking was considered pretty normal, and my folks—my dad especially—subscribed to that philosophy. As I once heard a preacher say, "He applied the rod of correction to the seat of my understanding."

What I understood from those experiences was that there was a cost to wrong behavior, and that cost could be avoided by right behavior. What I didn't understand was that the corrective discipline my parents applied was actually a proof of their love for me. It certainly didn't feel that way at the time, but I now know with great certainty that it absolutely was. Even Solomon understood this, for he wrote:

> For whom the LORD loves He disciplines,
> Just as a father disciplines the son in whom
> he delights.
>
> Proverbs 3:12

A good earthly father disciplines his beloved child in order to correct wrong behavior, and so does the Lord with the child He loves. And we see that discipline unfold as God responds to the idolatry that has been birthed in Solomon's heart due to his many wives and their influence on him:

> Now the LORD was angry with Solomon because his heart had turned away from the LORD, the God of Israel, who had appeared to him twice, and had commanded him regarding this thing, that he was not to follow other gods; but he did not comply with what the LORD had commanded. So the LORD said to Solomon, "Since you have done this, and you have not kept My covenant and My statutes, which I have commanded you, I will certainly tear the kingdom away from you, and will give it to your servant. However, I will not do it in your days, only for the sake of your father David; but I will tear it away from the hand of your son. Yet I will not tear away all the kingdom, but I will give one tribe to your son for the sake of My servant David, and for the sake of Jerusalem, which I have chosen." (1 Kings 11:9–13)

This is now the fourth time God has communicated with the king—and the progression of God's words is just as tragic as Solomon's journey. James Smith in *The Books of History* breaks them down this way:

At the start in a dream (3:5–14)—offering God's promised provision of wisdom and more

During temple construction by a prophet (6:11–13)—giving the promise that God would dwell there if Solomon was faithful

At the height of prosperity in a dream (9:1–9)—warning Solomon against the danger of spiritual failure

At the time of his apostasy (11:11–13)—declaring that the kingdom would be taken away as a consequence of Solomon's idolatry

That was the penalty for Solomon's spiritual failure: his family would lose the majority of the kingdom. How did that come about? Thomas Constable explains in *The Bible Knowledge Commentary*:

One of Solomon's subordinates (11:11) was Jeroboam, who tore the kingdom . . . from Solomon's son. The one tribe (v. 13) that God left in Rehoboam's hand was Judah. Actually two tribes were left (Judah and Benjamin) but Benjamin was small and the two became known as the Southern Kingdom of Judah. The tribe of Simeon had been given territory south of Judah but later at least part of Simeon moved north. . . . It was for David's sake that God tempered His judgment with mercy, and did not allow the split in Solomon's day. Whereas David had sinned against God deliberately, his heart remained devoted to the Lord. That is why his sin was not so serious as Solomon's. The greatest commandment is to love God with all one's heart (Deut. 6:5).

Not only would the kingdom be taken away, but it would be split in two—with the smaller remnant being ruled by Solomon's son. So, why such severe discipline? Because, perhaps, Solomon sinned despite the clearest possible revelation—God Himself speaking to him.

> Solomon lacked neither proof nor evidence of God's love and power. He had abundantly tasted God's love (1) by being chosen, contrary to what might have been expected, as David's successor; (2) in being given the special, personal name "Jedidiah" (i.e., "loved by the Lord"); (3) in receiving every benefit imaginable; and (4) in being visited by God twice for encouragement and admonition. He was given success in his endeavors beyond every expectation. These privileges should have created in Solomon a lifelong love and devotion of the deepest kind. But "the miraculously blessed heir of David, leader of the covenant people, has broken the most fundamental command of all: 'You shall have no other gods before me' (Exodus 20:3)." (*The Expositor's Bible Commentary*)

The Tragic Reality (Ecclesiastes 2:17)

Arguably the enduring consequence of Solomon's sin was that the joy, the wonder, the beauty of life was lost . . . whether in the grandeur of nature, or the presence of God, or the power of music, or whatever had been a source of joy to Solomon. Life had become jaded.

Life lost its magic and became a drudgery. And that may be the best explanation for the book of Ecclesiastes. Solomon, calling himself "the Preacher," wrote out of a heart that was filled with emptiness. Nothing mattered. Nothing helped. Nothing uplifted. The conclusion of the matter? Solomon, after writing about the emptiness ("vanity of vanities") and purposelessness of life, finally reached the absolute pit of his despair:

> So I hated life, for the work which had been done under the sun was unhappy to me; because everything is futility and striving after wind.

Once more, that despair can only be weighed against where Solomon started:

> Now Solomon loved the LORD, walking in the statutes of his father David. (1 Kings 3:3)

Looking back, everything that had brought light and joy was gone. There was only emptiness for this wise king who had become so desperately foolish.

The Sad Conclusion (1 Kings 11:41–43)

As a pastor I performed dozens of funerals, and some of the most difficult times in those already difficult times were when the deceased had lived a profligate and self-destructive life. How do you reflect on a life that wasn't well lived?

Usually the funeral director would hand me a 3" × 5" card with the particulars of the person's life—but that always felt unsatisfying. In such cases, you have to almost set aside the deceased and just present the gospel to those in attendance.

At the end of Solomon's story, the narrator of 1 Kings gives us the 3" × 5" card on his life—and it's decidedly uninspiring.

> Now the rest of the acts of Solomon and whatever he did, and his wisdom, are they not written in the Book of the Acts of Solomon? So the time that Solomon reigned in Jerusalem over all Israel was forty years. Then Solomon lay down with his fathers and was buried in the city of his father David, and his son Rehoboam reigned in his place. (11:41–43)

The disastrous condition of the divided kingdom would begin during the reign of Rehoboam and continue through those who followed him. And in a sense, even to this day, Israel is longing for a return to the golden age of Solomon. But it won't return until David's greater Son—Jesus—returns. David's son ultimately failed, but David's greater Son will not fail.

And in that moment when the true King comes, the world will finally be able to truly sing the words that Isaac Watts wrote in 1719. They're words we tend to sing at Christmas, but they aren't words that speak of Jesus's first coming . . . they speak of His second coming:

> Joy to the world! The Lord is come;
> Let earth receive her King;
> Let every heart prepare Him room,
> And heaven and nature sing,
> And heaven and nature sing,
> And heaven, and heaven and nature sing.

He rules the world with truth and grace,
And makes the nations prove
The glories of His righteousness,
And wonders of His love,
And wonders of His love,
And wonders, wonders of His love.

Questions for Personal Reflection or Group Discussion

1. Solomon ignored the spiritual danger of pagan, foreign wives and paid the price for it. What are some ways we can be pulled aside into wrong thinking about God and His instructions to us?

2. What is the "slippery slope" concept? Do you believe it's a real thing? It could be argued that Solomon's first marriage (to Pharaoh's daughter) placed his feet on a slippery slope that resulted in his hundreds of other marriages. How can we avoid getting caught on such a slippery slope?

3. What might a funeral-home 3" × 5" card say about you and your life? If it would be negative, what might you do now to prevent such an outcome?

4. Like the tragic consequences of Solomon's spiritual failures and their effects upon the nation, what might be some long-range effects of our choices—even in our children and grandchildren?

CONCLUSION
The Who Is the Why

There's a passage found in the book of Jeremiah that I feel speaks directly to Solomon's story—even though it was written long after his death. It's Jeremiah 9:23–24:

> This is what the LORD says: "Let no wise man boast of his wisdom, nor let the mighty man boast of his might, nor a rich man boast of his riches; but let the one who boasts boast of this, that he understands and knows Me, that I am the LORD who exercises mercy, justice, and righteousness on the earth; for I delight in these things," declares the LORD.

In Solomon's story, we've seen his wondrous wisdom, his remarkable military might (with his horses and chariots), and his extravagant wealth. Yet along the way he lost contact with his God—the one who was the ultimate source of all those blessings. It's a sad and truly tragic story indeed.

So, having considered the rise and fall of one of Israel's greatest kings and the wisest man of his generation, where does that leave us? With the reminder Jesus gave to the people of His generation: "Something greater than Solomon is here" (Matthew 12:42).

Solomon experienced—and abused—extraordinary blessings. Are we very different? In fact, we have a blessing Solomon could never have imagined. We have the blessing of the Holy Spirit dwelling in our lives, not to mention that we have the completed Scriptures as well. While we may feel comfortable taking shots at Solomon for his failures despite the light of great revelation, we've been blessed with even greater light through relationship with Jesus.

So then . . .

Why can we have wisdom?

Why can we avoid the traps of consumptive materialism?

Why can we have meaningful monogamous marriages?

Why can we live full, meaningful lives whether we have little or much?

The why is wrapped up in who we know—Jesus. Nothing else and no one else is able to meet the deepest needs of our lives and the deepest longing of our hearts. The challenge for us, as the writer of the letter to the Hebrews encourages us, is to be

looking only at Jesus, the originator and perfecter of the faith, who for the joy set before Him endured the cross, despising the shame, and has sat down at the right hand of the throne of God. (12:2)

In the old gospel song, Anna B. Warner reminds us:

Jesus loves me! This I know,
For the Bible tells me so;

Little ones to Him belong;
They are weak, but He is strong.

Jesus loves me still today,
Walking with me on my way,
Wanting as a friend to give
Light and love to all who live.

Yes, Jesus loves me!
Yes, Jesus loves me!
Yes, Jesus loves me!
The Bible tells me so.

We won't find what we seek in accumulating things or wealth or even human relationships. We find it in Him . . . the One who gave Himself for us. This is the root of true wisdom—Jesus is enough.

BIBLIOGRAPHY

Edersheim, Alfred. *Bible History: Old Testament.* 7th edition. Peabody, MA: Hendrickson Academic, 1994. *Bible History* first published in 7 volumes 1876–1887.

France, R. T., George H. Guthrie, J. Daryl Charles, Tom Thatcher, and Alan F. Johnson. *Hebrews–Revelation.* The Expositor's Bible Commentary, edited by Tremper Longman III and David E. Garland, vol. 13. Revised edition. Grand Rapids, MI: Zondervan, 2006.

Jamieson, Robert, Andrew Robert Fausset, and David Brown. *Jamieson, Fausset, and Brown's Commentary on the Whole Bible.* Grand Rapids, MI: Zondervan, 1961. First published 1871.

McCasland, David. *Eric Liddell: Pure Gold.* Grand Rapids, MI: Discovery House, 2001.

Smith, James E. *The Books of History.* Old Testament Survey Series. Joplin, MO: College Press Publishing Company, 1995.

Walvoord, John, and Roy B. Zuck, eds. *The Bible Knowledge Commentary: Old Testament.* Colorado Springs, CO: David C. Cook, 1983.

Wenham, G. J., J. A. Motyer, D. A. Carson, and R. T. France, eds. *The New Bible Commentary*. 21st Century Edition. Downers Grove, IL: InterVarsity Press, 1994.

Wiersbe, Warren W. *The Bible Exposition Commentary: New Testament*, vol. 1. Colorado Springs, CO: Victor Books, 2003.

————. *Wiersbe's Expository Outlines on the Old Testament*. Colorado Springs, CO: Victor Books, 1993.

Youngblood, Ronald F., Richard D. Patterson, and Hermann J. Austel. *1 Samuel–2 Kings*. The Expositor's Bible Commentary, edited by Tremper Longman III and David E. Garland, vol. 3. Revised edition. Grand Rapids, MI: Zondervan, 2009.